The
ROOTS
of Terrorism

Other titles in the Democracy and Terrorism Series,
Edited by Peter R. Neumann

DEMOCRACY AND TERRORISM
Leonard Weinberg

CONFRONTING TERRORISM
Peter R. Neumann

The
ROOTS
of Terrorism

Edited by **Louise Richardson**

Routledge
Taylor & Francis Group
New York London

Routledge is an imprint of the
Taylor & Francis Group, an informa business

Published in 2006 by
Routledge
Taylor & Francis Group
270 Madison Avenue
New York, NY 10016

Published in Great Britain by
Routledge
Taylor & Francis Group
2 Park Square
Milton Park, Abingdon
Oxon OX14 4RN

© 2006 by Taylor & Francis Group, LLC
Routledge is an imprint of Taylor & Francis Group

Printed in the United States of America on acid-free paper
10 9 8 7 6 5 4 3 2 1

International Standard Book Number-10: 0-415-95437-1 (Hardcover) 0-415-95438-X (Softcover)
International Standard Book Number-13: 978-0-415-95437-2 (Hardcover) 978-0-415-95438-9 (Softcover)

informa
Taylor & Francis Group
is the Academic Division of Informa plc.

Visit the Taylor & Francis Web site at
http://www.taylorandfrancis.com

and the Routledge Web site at
http://www.routledge-ny.com

Contents

Editors

Book Editor

Louise Richardson is executive dean of the Radcliffe Institute for Advanced Study at Harvard University, Cambridge. She coordinated the working groups on the underlying factors of terrorism at the International Summit on Democracy, Terrorism, and Security, and lectures widely on terrorism and counterterrorism to a wide range of international and domestic media and political, military, intelligence, academic, community, and alumni organizations.

Dr. Richardson holds positions on numerous international advisory boards including Club de Madrid, in Spain; Humanities Institute of Ireland; and the National Academy of Sciences Study Committeee on Technical and Privacy Dimensions of Information for Terrorism Prevention. Authoring over 20 monographs, edited volumes, articles, and chapters, she has written for *New England Journal of Medicine* and *Harvard International Review*. Her most recent book is *What Terrorists Want: Understanding the Enemy Containing the Threat* (Random House, 2006).

A lecturer on law at Harvard Law School, Dr. Richardson is also a senior lecturer in government at Harvard University. She has won various awards for her teaching including Award for Teaching Excellence from the Bok Center, as well as awards from the American Political Science Association and Pi Sigma Alpha, the Levenson Prize, and the Abramson Award, all from Harvard University. Dr. Richardson has also received various research and travel awards from the Ford Foundation, The Milton Fund, and The United States Institute of Peace.

Dr. Richardson holds a Ph.D. and M.A. in government from Harvard University, an M.A. in political science from the University of California, Los Angeles, as well as a B.A. and M.A. in history from University of Dublin, Trinity College, Ireland.

Series Editor

Peter R. Neumann is director of the Centre for Defence Studies at King's College London. Prior to this appointment, he was the Leverhulme research fellow in international terrorism at the Department of War Studies at King's College. He served as academic director of the Club de Madrid's *International Summit on Democracy, Terrorism and Security* in Madrid in March 2005, and acted as senior advisor to the *National Policy Forum on Terrorism, Security and America's Purpose*, which took place in Washington, D.C. in September 2005.

Dr. Neumann authored *Britain's Long War* (Palgrave Macmillan, 2003), the most comprehensive assessment of British strategy in the Northern Ireland conflict, and has written numerous articles on strategic terrorism, intelligence and counterterrorism in some of the foremost academic journals, including *The Journal of Strategic Studies, Orbis, Studies in Conflict and Terrorism*, and *Terrorism and Political Violence*. Shorter pieces have been published in the *International Herald Tribune*, the *New York Times*, the *Baltimore Sun*, and many others.

Currently working on a book on counterterrorism provisionally entitled *Democracy's Dilemma*, which will be released with IB Tauris in early 2007, Dr. Neumann is a member of the Club de Madrid's advisory board, and holds a Fellowship of the British Royal Society of Arts.

He obtained a Ph.D. in war studies from King's College London, and an M.A. in political science from the Free University of Berlin.

Before becoming an academic, Dr. Neumann worked as a journalist, serving as the London bureau chief of Germany's main radio news network, BLR. He was a news editor and reporter for Berlin's two most popular radio stations, RTL and RS2 radio.

Contributors

John L. Esposito is professor of religion and international affairs and founding director of the Center for Muslim–Christian Understanding at Georgetown University in Washington, D.C.

Atanas Gotchev is professor of international relations at the University of National and World Economy in Sofia, Bulgaria. Currently, he is a World Bank consultant on governance issues in the Caucuses Republics of the Russia's Southern Federal District.

Ted Robert Gurr is distinguished professor at the University of Maryland. He was founder of the Polity project, tracking democratization worldwide, and the Minorities at Risk project, monitoring 300 communal groups in conflict.

Nasra Hassan was born in Pakistan and, having worked in the Middle East, the Balkans, and Central Asia, is currently based with an international organization in Vienna, Austria.

Mark Juergensmeyer is professor of sociology and religious studies and director of the Orfalea Center of Global and International Studies at the University of California, Santa Barbara.

Jerrold M. Post is professor of psychiatry, political psychology, and international affairs and director of the Political Psychology Program at George Washington University in Washington, D.C.

Louise Richardson is executive dean of the Radcliffe Institute for Advanced Study at Harvard University, Cambridge. She coordinated the working groups on the underlying factors of terrorism at the International Summit on Democracy, Terrorism, and Security.

Olivier Roy is professor at the *Ecole des Hautes Etudes en Sciences Sociales* in Paris. He is the author of *Globalized Islam* (New York: Columbia University Press, 2004).

Ignacio Sánchez-Cuenca is associate professor of political science and sociology at the Juan March Institute and the Universidad Complutense, both in Madrid, Spain.

Gabriel (Gabi) Sheffer is professor of political science at the Hebrew University of Jerusalem. He was also director of the Leonard Davis Institute for International Relations at Hebrew University, and editor of the *Jerusalem Journal of International Relations*.

Michael S. Stohl is chair and professor in the Department of Communication at the University of California, Santa Barbara. His research focuses on political communication with special reference to terrorism, human rights, and global relations.

Leonard Weinberg is Foundation Professor of Political Science at the University of Nevada and served as a consultant to the United Nations Office for the Prevention of Terrorism. He is senior editor of the journal *Democracy and Security*.

Foreword

When the Club de Madrid hosted the International Summit on Democracy, Terrorism, and Security in Madrid in March 2005, the aim was to bring together the most important stakeholders in the debate about how democracies should confront the threat of terrorism. We believed that the debate among political leaders, policymakers, and expert practitioners had been incomplete at best and that it was important to provide a global forum in which all those who had something to contribute could sit around the table and talk to each other.

A first result of this process of dialogue was what we called the Madrid Agenda, released on the last day of the conference. Drawing on the various contributions made by the summit's participants, the document outlined the principles and ideas around which a pragmatic consensus in the fight against terrorism could be built. I was heartened by the fact that even the most hard-nosed antiterrorism practitioners—senior members of the intelligence services, army generals, and police chiefs—agreed that maintaining the rule of law, respecting human rights, and promoting democracy were all essential in making the struggle against terrorism effective in the long run.

Another point that came across very clearly was the need for our response against terrorism to be comprehensive. Even though law enforcement agencies have to be given the powers required to prevent terrorist attacks and to protect the lives of innocents, the summit participants were unanimous in their view that we must go further. As the Madrid Agenda states, "International institutions, governments and civil society should also address the underlying risk factors that provide terrorists with support and recruits."

Looking at the root causes of terrorism, however, is not as uncontroversial as it seems. Some dismiss it as simplistic; others even believe it is an effort to justify terrorism. I could not disagree more strongly. As the various contributions in this volume show, those who research the roots of terrorism are conscious that no single cause exists; instead, we are dealing with a complex, multifaceted problem that requires an equally sophisticated response. Indeed, if our attempts at addressing the roots of terrorism have been simplistic, it is probably because we have not done enough to understand them.

Furthermore, finding out why people become terrorists has nothing to do with excusing their crimes. On the contrary, to better appreciate the roots of terrorism strikes me as the most obvious starting point for how to construct our range of responses. It is about mapping what Louise Richardson once described as the "enabling environment" in which terrorism thrives. Doing so will allow us to draw on a much wider range of resources and will enable us to employ these in a more targeted way. In other words, rather than undermining it, such work will help to make the fight against terrorism more effective.

The Madrid Summit was held on the first anniversary of the train bombings in Madrid in 2004, and it was the memory of those terrible attacks that spurred our efforts. Even back then, I was convinced that the process of global engagement, dialogue and action that was begun in Madrid must continue. Following the recent bombings in London, Sharm-el-Sheikh and Bali, it is more necessary than ever. This book is an important part of that effort. I strongly commend it to every serious student of the topic.

Mary Robinson
Vice President of the Club de Madrid
Former President of Ireland

1

The Roots of Terrorism: An Overview

Louise Richardson

In June 2005 White House advisor Karl Rove criticized what he described as the effort of liberals after the attacks of September 11, 2001, to understand the terrorists.[1] In so saying, Rove was reflecting a common predilection to equate understanding terrorism with sympathy for terrorists. Like the sixty-five academics who deliberated together on the underlying causes of terrorism for several months and who convened in Madrid on the first anniversary of the Atocha train bombings, I reject this view. We believe that only by understanding the forces leading to the emergence of terrorism—the root causes, in other words—can we hope to devise a successful long-term counterterrorist strategy.

As the contributions to this volume demonstrate, the search for the underlying causes of terrorism is a complicated endeavor. The difficulty of the task must serve as an inducement to sustained and rigorous research on the subject—not as invitation to throw in the towel and deal simply with the symptoms that present themselves. Policy makers, faced with pressures for immediate action to deal with a formidable threat, can be forgiven for seeking a rapid reaction plan. The role of academics, on the other hand, is to ensure that the plans they reach for are based on a deep-seated understanding of the nature of the threat they face.

The search for the cause of terrorism, like the search for a cure for cancer, is not going to yield a single definitive solution. But as with any disease, an effective cure will be dependent on the accurate diagnosis of the multiplicity of risk factors as well as their interactions with one another. The cure is likely to be almost as complicated as the disease, entailing a combination of alleviating the risk factors, blocking the interactions between them, and building the body's resilience to exposure. Above all, it will focus first and foremost on preventing the spread of the disease.

The working definition of *terrorism* employed by this group—in the absence of an agreed international definition—is contained in the U.S. Code: "Premeditated, politically motivated violence perpetrated against non-combatant targets by sub-national groups or clandestine agents, usually intended to influence an audience."[2] Terrorism, in fact, is a complex and multivariate phenomenon. It appears in many different forms in many parts of the world in pursuit of many different objectives. It occurs in democracies, autocracies, and transitional states and in developed, underdeveloped, and developing economies. It is practiced by adherents of many religions and by adherents of none. What all terrorist groups have in common is that they are weaker than their enemies and that they are prepared deliberately to murder noncombatants in furtherance of their objectives. The adoption of terrorism as a tactic to effect political change is, therefore, a deliberate choice.

Terrorist groups differ from one another in important ways. They differ in the nature of their ideology and in the specificity of their political objectives. They differ in their relationship to religion and to the communities from which they derive support. They also differ in the trajectory of their violence. Historically, for example, most terrorist groups were domestic, and others started locally and went global; recently, however, global conflicts seem to inspire local groups to terrorism.

One of the most obvious difficulties in identifying a cause or causes of terrorism is that terrorism is a microphenomenon. Metaexplanations cannot be used successfully to explain microphenomena. Take the case of social revolutionary movements in Europe in the 1970s for example. Their behavior was attributed to the alienation of the young whose postwar idealism was thwarted by capitalist materialism. But if this alienation was the cause, then why were there not many more terrorists? Alienation was widespread, but terrorism, fortunately, had relatively few adherents. Alienation alone, therefore, cannot stand as the cause of their terrorism.

Nationalist terrorism, on the other hand, has been more broadly based. Ethnonationalist groups have resorted to terrorism all over the world from Northern Ireland, Spain, and Corsica to Turkey, Chechnya, Sri Lanka, India, and the Middle East. But if nationalism were the cause of their terrorism, then why have other ethnic and nationalist groups—who do not occupy a territory consistent with their sense of identity—not also resorted to terrorism? Nationalism can provide a sense of grievance and a unifying and legitimizing aspiration, but it cannot alone explain why a group seeks to realize their nationalist goal through terrorist violence as opposed to other forms of political action.

The contributors to this volume reflect a range of academic disciplines from psychologist to sociologist, from economist to political scientist and historian. None claim for their fields a monopoly on insight into the root causes of terrorism. On the contrary, each concedes the need for several approaches to the problem. Different fields, however, tend to focus on particular levels of analysis. These have been broadly divided into individual, political, economic, and cultural factors. I first review the arguments made by the contributors and then extrapolate the policy prescriptions from their analysis before spelling out a research agenda that would advance our understanding of the crucial question of the roots of terrorism.

Underlying Causes of Terrorism

At the level of the individual, psychologists have long argued that there is no particular terrorist personality and that the notion of terrorists as crazed fanatics is not consistent with the plentiful empirical evidence available. Jerrold Post points out that terrorists are psychologically normal in the sense of not being clinically psychotic; they are neither depressed nor severely emotionally disturbed. Instead, he advocates an analysis of the crucial concept of collective identity where group, organizational, and social psychology provide more analytical power than individual psychology. He argues that the sociocultural context determines the balance between collective and individual identity and in particular the manner in which terrorist recruits subordinate their individual identity to that of the collective. He points to the importance of distinguishing leaders from followers and of understanding the crucial role of the leader in providing a sense-making message to the followers. Post also stresses the importance of group dynamics and the manner in which groups may make riskier decisions than individuals. He points out that if the path to leadership in an organization is through violence, then the group will be pushed inexorably toward greater and greater levels of violence irrespective of what individuals may think.

Nasra Hassan also focuses on individuals and in particular on individual suicide jihadis. She interviewed the families and friends of 250 suicide bombers from a variety of conflicts and compares the appeal and the implementation of the tactic among the different religious and secular groups who employ it. Like other contributors to this volume she challenges the view that madrassa and mosque schools are the chief generator of suicide jihadis, suggesting instead the broader environment and the volunteers selected for the special training camps. Though she cites certain essential elements like loyalty to a charismatic figure and preexisting grievances against an outgroup, by examining the many differences among the various suicide terrorist campaigns, the mixture of religious and political motive and rhetoric, and the style of training and method of deployment Hassan implicitly challenges the notion that there is any one simple cause of even this particular terrorist tactic or even a shared profile of the suicide jihadist.

Where psychologists and writers seek explanation at the individual and group level, political scientists bring the tools of their trade to bear in attempting to establish lines first of correlation and then causation between the outbreak of terrorism and the nature of the political environment in which the violence takes place. Recognizing the myriad different types of terrorism, Ignacio Sánchez-Cuenca focuses his analysis on revolutionary movements. These were the movements that bedeviled several wealthy western democracies in the mid-1970s and early 1980s. They include the Red Brigades and Prima Linea in Italy, the Red Army Faction in Germany, First of October Antifascist Resistance Group (GRAPO) in Spain, the Revolutionary Organization 17 November in Greece, FP 25 Abril in Portugal, and Action Directe in France. In a multivariate analysis with twenty-one countries, Sánchez-Cuenca finds that by far the most powerful predictor of the lethality of violence is past political instability. He uses what he terms a *political selection model* to demonstrate why revolutionary violent groups emerged in many developed countries in the '70s and '80s but only evolved into terrorist groups in a handful of cases. He found that terrorist groups emerged in states that had experienced past political instability and had powerful social movements in the '60s, had engaged in counterproductive repression, and had also seen an emergence of fascist terrorism. While Sánchez-Cuenca believes this model could probably also explain the emergence of ethnonationalist terrorism in Spain and Northern Ireland, he has no illusions that it could be employed convincingly in cases of international terrorism in which the unit of observation is not a clearly defined state. His analysis speaks to the wisdom of disaggregating the very broad concept of terrorism and focusing instead on particular types of terrorist groups.

Leonard Weinberg also chooses to narrow his analysis. He examines the political sources of terrorism in democracies. In thinking about the domestic political causes he retains political scientist Martha Crenshaw's distinction between *permissive* and *instigating* factors.[3] The weakness of analyzing along the lines of permissive causes is demonstrated implicitly by Sánchez-Cuenca: The same permissive factors can exist in several states but only produce terrorism in some. Another weakness correctly identified by Weinberg is that, thanks to new forms of technology, behavior can be quickly diffused and terrorist campaigns can spread from one country to another in spite of differences in the political conditions of those countries.

Weinberg subjects to empirical testing several arguments found in the literature on the relationship between terrorism and democracy. He finds that outbreaks of terrorism are not the exclusive preserve of transitional democracies. He points out that in fact, although terrorism can be present at the creation of democracy, the failure of democracies to respond forcibly also has brought about their demise, as in Uruguay, Argentina, and Turkey. He also demonstrates that longevity in no way insulates democracies from outbreaks of domestic terrorism.

After exploring the explanatory power of temporal permissive explanations Weinberg turns to structural ones. He refers to data analysis—again limited to western democracies—indicating that the greater the degree of ethnic diversity and the greater the degree of political fragmentation in the polity, the higher the incidence of terrorism. Conversely, the more evenly distributed the income and the better the record in protecting civil rights, the lower the incidence of terrorism. He recognizes the problems of causality here, of course, as states that have had fewer threats from terrorists may have better protections for civil liberties as a consequence, not a cause. He concludes that instigating factors like radicalization and their interaction with the behavior of the state are more likely to be helpful in understanding outbreaks of terrorism.

The relative recency of transnational terrorism means that data collection is at a much more rudimentary stage. Nevertheless, Weinberg believes that broad-based explanations such as the structure of the international system or globalization are not consistent with the evidence. The unipolar system as an explanatory variable is undermined by the presence of terrorism under multipolar as well as unipolar international distributions of power. He also uses empirical analysis to challenge the explanatory power of globalization, arguing that an examination of terrorist incidents suggests that more incidents take place among those at the bottom of the globalization scale, secondly among those at the top and the least between those at opposite ends. That is, most terrorist attacks are committed by citiens of countries a the bottom of the globalization index against citizens of countries also at the bottom of the index. When citizens of highly globalized countries are victims their attackers tend to come from other highly globalized societies. Attacks by citizens of countries at the bottom of the index against citizens of countries at the top are less common. These findings, however, again speak to the need to disaggregate among different types of groups because the incidence of Islamist terrorism suggests a different result, as seen in the contribution of Atanas Gotchev.

Gotchev, an economist, explores the downside effects of globalization as a cause of terrorism. He shows how the inequitable distribution of the positive effectives of globalization across countries provides both incentives and opportunities to organize, finance, and carry out terrorist acts. He does not argue that globalization causes terrorism but rather that it too can creative a permissive environment for its occurrence. He points out that globalization has increased inequalities and social polarization both within and between states and that this in turn leads to demands for political change. Moreover, the spread of western culture and the need to adapt to take advantage of the benefits of globalization provoke political and cultural resistance and an emphasis on differences. Gotchev argues that globalization also fosters the development of new minorities by facilitating the movement of labor. These in turn may provide both logistical and financial support as well as human capital for the terrorist groups. He goes on to argue that globalization diminishes the power of the nation state by constraining the state's ability to control its economy and by enabling a proliferation of nongovernmental organizations. Finally, he argues that globalization provides both new methods and new easily accessible targets for terrorists.

Gotchev does not argue, contra Weinberg, that globalization causes terrorism but rather that it facilitates its emergence. Globalization then falls into Crenshaw's category of a permissive cause of terrorism. Gabi Sheffer takes this argument a step further by examining this *other* that is produced by globalization. He explores the diaspora and offers a classification of the various components of the *other*. He explores the many behavioral and organizational differences among different elements of the diaspora and assesses the degree of intensity of their violence both in their adoptive and originating countries. The link between diasporas and terrorism is not hard to find. He argues that twenty-seven of the fifty most active contemporary terrorist organizations are either part of a diaspora or are supported by one—though he would not, of course, challenge the view that most members of diaspora communities utterly reject the use of terrorism to redress their grievances.

Sociologist Ted Gurr also explores some of the many complex linkages between economic factors and terrorism. Arguing that terrorism is a choice made by groups waging conflict rather than an automatic response to deprivation, he points out that the perpetrators of the September 11, 2001, atrocity in the United States were middle class and well educated. They were also products of societies undergoing profound socioeconomic changes in which opportunities for political expression were sharply curtailed. In addition, they were all recruited by Islamists committed to jihad against the West.

Gurr contends that objective poverty is not a direct cause of terrorism, though it can contribute indirectly to the outbreak of terrorism in many ways. He argues quite convincingly that inequalities, or relative deprivation, are more important than poverty as a source of terrorism. This also helps to account for the common observation that leaders of terrorist movements, like leaders of organizations, generally tend to be more highly educated and of a higher socioeconomic status than their followers and those in their communities. Ethnonationalist terrorism in particular can be linked to discrimination on the basis of ethnic identity, though not all instances of ethnic discrimination lead to terrorism. Rapid socioeconomic change also serves as a risk factor for terrorism. This is because of the instability it generates and the associated dislocations produced.

His argument then is that, rather than poverty, structured inequalities within countries facilitate the emergence of terrorism and that rapid socioeconomic change feeds this process. When these factors interact with the restrictions on political rights, disadvantaged groups are what Gurr calls "ripe for recruitment." As Weinberg and Michael Stohl also notice, semirepressive state reactions often contribute to the evolution from political mobilization to terrorism because of their inconsistent mix of repression and reform. Finally, like Sheffer, Gurr explores the relationship between terrorism and conventional crime as the need to finance the former often draws the terrorist toward the latter.

Turning away from an examination of economic and political to explore cultural and religious causes, our authors focus on Islam and jihad. John Esposito provides a historical analysis of the emergence of what he calls *political Islam,* more often referred to as Islamism or Islamic fundamentalism, and in so doing makes the crucial distinction between mainstream and extremist movements. He concludes that terrorists like Osama bin Laden are driven not by religion but by political and economic grievances; however, they draw on a tradition of religious extremism to legitimize their actions. They ignore classical Islam's criteria for a just war, recognizing no limits but their own. They also reject classical Islam's regulations regarding a valid jihad with its insistence on the protection of noncombatants and the proportionate use of violence. Esposito argues that the primary causes—

which are socioeconomic and political to varying degrees in different contexts—are obscured by the religious language and extremism used by extremists.

Olivier Roy explores the explanatory issue of *deculturation* as a cause of Islamic terrorism. An empirical examination of the perpetrators of Islamic violence in Western Europe, he argues, suggests they are part of a broad supranational network operating in the West that is disconnected from any discrete territorial base. Contrary to popular opinion Roy points out that their backgrounds have little to do with traditional religious education or even particular conflicts in the Middle East: They became born-again Muslims in the West—not in radical mosques but rather in the framework of a group of similarly uprooted local friends. They have very little connection to the real Muslim world or to the world of their parents. They were in effect rebels in search of a cause when Islamism presented itself. He concludes that their radicalization has nothing whatever to do with Islam as a culture and everything to do with "deculturation and individualization." He sees them, in essence, as another example of religious revivalism with a global perception of the state of the *ummah*, that is, the global community of Islam. If Roy is correct, then the task of governments is to accept Islam as a Western religion among many others and not as the expression of an ethnocultural community. It means working to undermine foreign connections and instead integrating Muslims and community leaders on a pluralist basis.

Mark Juergensmeyer looks more broadly at all religions and their relationship to terrorism. He agrees with Esposito that underlying economic social and political grievances—rather than religion—are the initial problem but points out that these secular concerns are now being expressed through rebellious religious ideologies, which makes then more intractable. These grievances provide a sense of alienation, marginalization, and social frustration but they are being articulated in religious terms, are being seen through religious images, and are being organized by religious leaders through religious institutions. Religion then brings new aspects to the conflict. It provides personal rewards, vehicles for social mobilization, organizational networks, and, more importantly, a justification for violence. Juergensmeyer argues that religion does not cause terrorism but problematizes it because it absolutizes the conflict, thereby making its resolution enormously more difficult.

The contributors to this volume do not produce a set of causes to be fixed so as to end terrorism. Rather, through an analysis of specific cases, concepts, and raw data they indicate a set of risk factors for the emergence of terrorism. The risk factors alone will not cause terrorism; they need to be ignited by particular events, policies, or leaders that mobilize the disaffection they generate into violent action. Ameliorating these risk factors is not a short-term process and so is unlikely to have immediate results in the campaign against terrorism, but over the longer term this action is likely to have significant benefits throughout these societies and indirectly to reduce support for a resort to terrorist action.

Policy Recommendations

Effective counterterrorist policies likely will address both the underlying and the proximate causes of the violence and will combine long-term developmental strategies with short-term and often coercive responses. It is imperative, however, that in their haste to secure short-term success against terrorists, governments should not lose sight of the longer-term goals—that the implementation of the short-term measures does not undermine the achievement of the long-term objectives.

The long-term goal is to delegitimize the resort to terrorism as a means of effecting political change and to reduce the opportunities and incentives for doing so. It is to channel the effort to redress grievances into conventional politics. Action in furtherance of this aim is unlikely to appeal to currently practicing terrorists but over the long term is likely to undermine their ability to win recruits for their cause. A more immediate and closely related goal is to separate terrorists from the communities from which they derive support, to deny them means of recruiting new members, and to prevent the appeal of their ideology and their actions from spreading

An essential goal of long-term counterterrorism policy must be to reduce the reservoir of resentment that breeds support for the resort to terrorism. In working toward this goal, it is crucial to remember that the majority of the populations, and even the majority of political activists in societies that produce terrorism, are among the most powerful forces for securing stable and safe societies. Punitive policies, therefore, must be focused on the perpetrators of the violence. Esposito points out, for example, that a zero-tolerance approach to mainstream political Islamic movements not only will undermine civil society and the credibility of the West's commitment to democracy but also will produce the alienation that feeds the growth of terrorism. Mainstream movements, he argues, require engagement, whereas zero tolerance should be reserved for extremists. Stohl also reminds us how repressive action and denial of human rights on the part of the state can precipitate outbreaks of terrorist violence and that counterterrorist action, taken without regard for democratic principles and the rule of law, can serve to generate more terrorism.

Among the longer-term economic responses to terrorism are mitigating the impact of globalization or rapid socioeconomic change on vulnerable segments of the population in developing countries. Aid and investment, therefore, should be targeted to those most directly affected to enable them to influence the nature and pace of development. Those attempting to counter terrorism should be prepared to help finance socioeconomic policies that promote the growth of a middle class and women's literacy and education. A burgeoning middle class and the political and economic participation of women can serves as breaks on the development of extremism. Governments must be encouraged to reduce gross inequalities and group discrimination and to integrate marginalized groups into political and economic activity. Educational opportunities must be enhanced, but this must go hand in hand with economic development to ensure that employment opportunities are available for those so educated. The West should be prepared to provide alternatives to traditional Islamic education that fails to provide the tools for participation in modernizing societies. The need to integrate marginalized groups is not, however, limited to developing countries. On the contrary, the alienation of diaspora communities in the wealthiest countries in the world remains a real vulnerability and must be addressed.

Finally, those of us in the U.S. must engage in a war of ideas with the extremist ideologies. We should be able to mobilize local moderates to our side in this campaign, but we will only be able to do so successfully if our rhetoric at home is matched by our action on the ground. In this effort we should be prepared to support moderate Islamic scholarship and political parties even when they are critical of our actions. We need to engage in a vigorous campaign of public diplomacy to make our case to the populations that produce terrorists. We are only likely to be successful in the effort if we can demonstrate that our commitment to liberal ideals and the rule of law is consistently applied and that we hold ourselves and our allies to the same standards as we hold others. We need to exploit new media technologies to engage in what Post calls a strategic communications program to address systematically the arguments against us and to counter the avenues through which extremists win recruits.

We should not have any illusions that success will come quickly. Many terrorist groups have ended their campaigns fairly quickly, but these were small isolated movements like the Red Army Faction (RAF), or movements effectively destroyed by police action like Revolutionary Organization 17 November or by ruthless suppression by the state, as in several Latin American countries. Other movements—especially those with close ties to their communities—have lasted a very long time. In societies in which, in Post's words, "hatred has been bred in the bone" and in which socialization begins at an early age and is reinforced and consolidated into an essential element of collective identity, no short-term solution exists. The goal, however, is not to turn the world into American cheerleaders. The only threshold the U.S. needs to reach will come from people not employing terrorism as a means to voice their frustrations, their objections to American policies or American influence on their societies.

Of course, more immediate steps can be and are being taken. These entail reducing the financial, material, and political resources of terrorist organizations and inhibiting their ability to move freely through enhanced border and customs controls. Several contributors speak to the need to investigate fraudulent charities and to otherwise disrupt the flow of money to terrorist groups. To these suggestions I add the need to review the foreign policies of governments with global influence with a view of how they advance a broader definition of the state's national interest. Westerners should be prepared to incorporate into the evaluation of our policies how they are perceived on the ground and whether, in the eyes of the populations whose confidence we are trying to acquire, our policies appear to be more consistent with our ideals than with the motives attributed to us by the extremists.

A concerted effort on our part to redress political conflicts that have been exploited by extremists will again undermine their efforts to win recruits. A resolution of the Israeli–Palestinian dispute or the dispute between India and Pakistan over Kashmir will not satisfy the extremists, but it will reduce the reservoir of resentment on which they feed. One of the big advantages of following these policy recommendations is that they have a myriad of benefits. Even if generous and strategically distributed development aid and a resolution of political conflicts did not undercut terrorism, as I have argued they would,[4] they have many other quite tangible benefits in the improvement to the quality of life of those affected.

Research Agenda

This book is far from being the last word on understanding the root causes of terrorism. As each of the contributors makes clear, there remains a great deal that we do not know and yet we need to know if we care to understand the terrorist threat. This book provides a detailed account of the permissive factors facilitating the emergence of terrorism. The proximate causes of terrorism are more obvious and are regularly stated publicly by the perpetrators of the violence. We know much less about the way the proximate and the permissive

causes interact with one another. We know they interact through the
leaders and their followers, but we have a lot to learn about how this
happens. In this sense, a great deal of research needs to be done on the
terrorist life cycle. In order to disrupt the path into terrorism and to
devise policies that inhibit potential recruits from joining, encourage
experienced recruits to leave, produce dissent within the group, and
undermine the internal authority of the leaders, we need to gather a
great deal more information about how the groups operate internally.
There is no substitute for primary research in this endeavor.

The proliferation of terrorist attacks and growing lethality of
terrorist violence inclines others to see terrorism as an ideology and
terrorists as a uniform mass of evildoers. They cannot usefully be
understood in this way. Each terrorist group must be understood in
its own context; the most successful counterterrorist strategy is likely
to be particularly geared to that group. That said, we need to have a
keener understanding of how groups are similar and how they are not.
Detailed, structured, focused comparisons based on intensive analysis of a range of movements are likely to enhance our understanding
both of individual groups and of the phenomenon more generally.

In this book we demonstrate that terrorism is not caused by
religion, globalization, political structures, or psychopaths. We do
argue, however, that political and economic inequalities and social
alienation are risk factors for the emergence of terrorism. Religion
can exacerbate the problem, as it can be used to legitimize the use
of violence to redress these political and socioeconomic grievances.
Once grievances are expressed in religious terms the conflict becomes
altogether more difficult to resolve. There is a lot we do not know
about the underlying causes of terrorism, but everything we do
know points to the importance of developing a long-term coordinated strategy that is consistent with our democratic principles and
in which short-term objectives are integrated with long-term goals. It
is both unwise and unnecessary to sacrifice liberal democratic values
to secure short-term security. On the contrary, the strongest weapons in our arsenal against terrorism are precisely the facets of our
society that appeal to the potential recruits for terrorists. And these
potential recruits—who come from the communities from which terrorists derive their support—should become the focus of counterterrorist policies. If we can help to redress the rampant economic inequi-
ties and sociopolitical marginalization in these communities we will
reduce both the opportunities and the incentives for the resort to terrorism, thereby constraining the growth and increasing the isolation
of terrorist groups. We can then focus our coercive policies on these
perpetrators of violence. These directed policies are far more likely

to be successful if they are based on a thorough understanding of the nature of the group being faced. A plan of action that involves mobilizing the moderates while integrating the marginalized and isolating the extremists is entirely consistent with the principles of democracy our governments were designed to defend in the first place.

Endnotes

1. Karl Rove (speech, Conservative Party of New York State, June 22, 2005).
2. U.S. Code, title 22, sec. 2656f(d).
3. Martha Crenshaw, "The Causes of Terrorism" *Comparative Politics*, Volume 13, No. 4, (July 1981) pp 379-400.
4. Louise Richardson, *What Terrorists Want: Understanding the Terrorist Threat*, John Murray, London, 2006.

Individual and
Psychological Roots

2

The Psychological Dynamics
of Terrorism[1]

Jerrold M. Post

Since the beginning of the modern era of terrorism, represented by the iconic event of the seizure of the Israeli Olympic village at the 1972 Munich Olympics by Black September terrorists, behavioral scientists have sought the holy grail of the *terrorist personality*. But these efforts have proven fruitless, for the label *terrorism* refers to an extremely complex and diverse phenomenon. In considering the psychology of right-wing, nationalist-separatist, social revolutionary, and religious fundamentalist terrorists—given how different their causes and perspectives are—these types are expected to differ markedly. So we should discuss terrorisms—plural—and terrorist psychologies—plural—rather than searching for a unified general theory explaining all terrorist behavior. In other words, there is not a one-size-fits-all explanation: The leadership and follower, group and organizational dynamics, and decision patterns will differ from group to group. And although psychology plays a crucial role in understanding terrorism, a comprehensive understanding of this complex phenomenon requires an interdisciplinary approach, incorporating knowledge from political, historical, cultural, economic, ideological, and religious scholarship. It is important to consider each terrorism in its own political, historical, and cultural context, since terrorism is a product of its own place and time. It is an attractive strategy to a diverse array of groups that have little else in common otherwise.

Explanations of terrorism at the level of individual psychology are insufficient in helping to understand why people become involved in terrorism. Indeed, it is not going too far to assert that terrorists are psychologically normal—that is, not clinically psychotic. They are not depressed and not severely emotionally disturbed, nor are they crazed fanatics. In fact, terrorist groups and organizations regularly weed out emotionally unstable individuals. They represent, after all, a security risk. Indeed, there is a multiplicity of individual motivations. For some, revenge is a primary motivation; for others, it is to give a sense of power to the powerless; for still others, it is to gain a sense of significance. Within each group can be found motivational differences among the members, each of whom is motivated to differing degrees by group interest versus self-serving actions, as well as by ideology.

There is a clear consensus that group, organizational, and social psychology—and not individual psychology—provide the greatest analytic power in understanding this complex phenomenon where collective identity is paramount. For some groups, especially nationalist-separatist terrorist groups, this collective identity is established extremely early so that *hatred is bred in the bone*. The importance of collective identity and the processes of forming and transforming collective identities cannot be overstated. This, in turn, emphasizes the sociocultural context, which determines the balance between collective and individual identity. Terrorists subordinate their individual identity to the collective identity so that what serves the group, organization, or network is of primary importance. Some of the themes following from this idea are explored in this chapter. In particular, I highlight a number of key dynamics and structures that are significant in understanding the psychological bases of terrorism and then outline a series of policy recommendations based on these insights.

Social and Generational Dynamics

The first important area of consideration is the social and generational dynamics of terrorist groups. The dynamics of nationalist-separatist terrorist groups, such as Euzakadi ta Askabasuna–Basque Fatherland and Liberty ETA of Spain's Basque region or the Palestinian group Fatah, differ dramatically from those of social-revolutionary terrorist groups, such as the Red Army Faction in Germany or Italy's Red Brigades. This is illustrated in a generational matrix (Figure 2.1).[2] The X in the upper left-hand cell indicates that individuals who are at one with parents loyal to the regime do not become terrorists. The lower left-hand cell shows individuals rebelling against their parents who are loyal to the regime. One of the Baader-Meinhoff terrorists once sardonically remarked, "This is the generation of corrupt old men who gave us Auschwitz and Hiroshima." One can make a case

	Parents' Relationship to Regime	
Youth's Relationship to Parents	**L**oyal	**D**isloyal amaged issident
Loyal	X	Nationalist-Separatist Terrorism ✓
Disloyal	Social Revolutionary Terrorism ✓	

Figure 2.1

that these dynamics apply to Osama bin Laden, who—in striking out at the Saudi regime, criticizing them for accepting occupation by the U.S. military of "the land of the two cities"—was striking out at the generation of his family that was loyal to the regime. So although bin Laden is a religious fundamentalist terrorist, he has the dynamics of a social revolutionary as well. In contrast, in the upper right-hand cell are the nationalist-separatist terrorists, carrying on the mission of their parents who are disloyal to, dissident to, or damaged by the regime. Whether in the pubs of Northern Ireland or the coffee houses in the Palestinian territories, they have heard of the economic injustice or of the lands stolen from their parents and grandparents. They are loyal to parents disloyal to the regime. For these groups in particular, hatred has been transmitted generationally.

The theme of loyalty to a family that has been damaged by the regime is well illustrated by Omar Rezaq, an Abu Nidal Organization terrorist tried in the federal district court in Washington D.C. in 1996.[3] I had the opportunity of interviewing Rezaq during my service as expert on terrorist psychology for the Department of Justice in connection with his trial for the federal crime of skyjacking. It was Rezaq who played a central role in seizing the Egypt Air plane that was forced down in Malta in 1985. He shot five hostages—two Israeli women and three Americans—before a botched SWAT team attack by Egyptian forces led to more than fifty casualties. Convicted of murder in a Malta court, Rezaq was given amnesty and was released after seven years of imprisonment. Subsequently, though, he was arrested by U.S. Federal Bureau of Investigation agents.

Rezaq epitomized the life and psychology of the nationalist-separatist terrorist. On the basis of some eight hours of interviews and the review of thousands of pages of documents, a coherent story emerged. The defendant assuredly did not believe that what he was doing was wrong: From boyhood on Rezaq had been socialized to be a heroic revolutionary fighting for the Palestinian nation. Demonstrating the generational transmission of hatred, his case can be considered emblematic of many from the ranks of ethnic–nationalist terrorist groups, from Northern Ireland to Palestine, from Armenia to the Basque region of Spain.

Rezaq's mother was eight years old and living in Jaffa when the 1948 Arab–Israeli War broke out, forcing her family to flee their home for the West Bank. The mother's displacement by Israel from her ancestral home was an event of crucial importance and became a key element in the family legend. Born in 1958, Rezaq spent his childhood in the West Bank village where his grandfather was a farmer. In 1967, the year he turned eight, the Arab–Israeli Six Day War broke out, and the family was forced to flee once again—this time to a refugee camp in Jordan. There, young Rezaq attended a school where his teachers were members of the Palestinian Liberation Organization (PLO). In 1968, the battle of Karameh occurred, in which Yasser Arafat led a group of Palestinian guerrillas in fighting a twelve-hour battle against superior Israeli forces, galvanizing the previously dispirited Palestinian population. The spirit of the revolution was everywhere, especially in the refugee camps, and the PLO became a rallying point. In Rezaq's words, "The revolution was the only hope."

In school, Rezaq was taught by a member of the PLO whom he came to idolize, that the only way to become a man was to join the revolution and to regain the lands taken away from his parents and grandparents. In the morning, he was exposed to a basic elementary school curriculum, and starting at age nine, in the afternoon he was given paramilitary training and ideological indoctrination. He joined Fatah when he was seventeen and subsequently became a member of the Abu Nidal Organization. When he carried out the skyjacking, it was the proudest moment of his life. He was fulfilling his destiny. He was carrying on his family's cause—a cause that had been *bred in the bone*.

This, incidentally, is also true for many militant Islamists, whose hatred often was steeped from childhood on in the mosques. Consider the following statement from an incarcerated Hamas terrorist:

> I came from a religious family which used to observe all the Islamic traditions. My initial political awareness came during the prayers at the mosque. That's where I was also asked to join religious classes. In the context of these studies, the Sheik used to inject some historical background in which he would tell us how we were effectively evicted from Palestine. The Sheik also used to explain to use the significance of the fact that there was a military outpost [of the Israeli Defense Forces] in the heart of the camp. He compared it to a cancer in the human body, which was threatening its very existence.[4]

It could be argued, therefore, that—whether they profess to be revolutionaries, to be religiously motivated or to be nationalist-separatists—the generational and social dynamics of potential terrorists have an important bearing on their attitudes and overall development.

Leaders and Followers

In addition to understanding the social dynamics of terrorist groups, it is important to distinguish leaders from followers. The role of the leader is crucial in drawing together alienated, frustrated individuals into a coherent organization. They provide a sense-making unifying message that conveys a religious, political, or ideological goal to their disparate followers. The leader plays a crucial role in identifying the external enemy as the cause, and drawing together into a collective identity otherwise dissimilar individuals who may be discontented and aggrieved, but who, without the powerful presence of the leader, would remain isolated and individually aggrieved. Hoffer, in *The True Believer*, speaks of the capacity of the hate-mongering leader to manipulate "the slime of discontented souls."[5] The hate-mongering leader—or political entrepreneur—also plays a crucial organizing role, as exemplified by bin Laden who has become a positive identification object for thousands of alienated Arab and Muslim youth. For them, he serves as the heroic avenger with the courage to stand up against the superpower. And in following his lead, the individual group member is seen as unselfish, altruistic, and heroic to the point of self-sacrifice. Equally significant—though less well understood—is the process by which followers enter the leadership echelon, because this dynamic is critical to the viability of the group. Systematic study of autobiographical accounts may help identify the salient features of this dynamic, which will be expected to differ from group to group.

Though it is easy to understand how a religious fundamentalist leader can use his religious authority to justify extreme acts to his followers, charismatic leaders can persuade their true-believer followers to carry out such acts in pursuit of a secular cause as well. This has been demonstrated by the willingness of members of the Kurdish separatist PKK (The Kurdistan Workers' Party) or the Sri Lankan Tamil Tigers (LTTE) to commit suicide terrorism for a nationalist cause. If anything, these examples reveal that the sway of a destructive charismatic leader is such that his followers uncritically accept the leader's views and follow his directions without further questioning.

In this context it is useful to look briefly at the dynamics of suicide terrorism, which is a function of a culture of martyrdom, the leader's decision to employ this tactic, and a supply of recruits willing to give their lives[6] in a "martyrdom operation" (see Nasra Hassan's contribution in this book). Social psychological forces are particularly important, leading Ariel Merari to speak of the "suicide terrorist production line" with first, the social contract established, and then the identification of the "living martyr," who accrues great prestige within the community, and, then in the culminating phase, the production of the final video.[7] After passing through these three phases, to back away from the final act of martyrdom would bring unbearable shame and humiliation. Thus, as with terrorist psychology in general, suicide terrorism is very much a function of group and collective psychology, not individual psychopathology. Furthermore, the case of suicide terrorism illustrates that the power of group dynamics cannot be overemphasized. As demonstrated by Semel and Minnix in their article on the so-called risky shift, a group can make a riskier decision than any individual in the group might make. If the path to leadership in the group is through extremism and violence, this inexorably pushes the group in that direction.[8]

The Terrorist Life Cycle

Terrorists differ according to their motivation, and their behavior also may vary according to the stage of their terrorist career. It is necessary, therefore, to unpack the life course of terrorists to consider the psychological processes they are undergoing at different points in their evolution as group members. What initially attracts a potential terrorist to the terrorist group differs from what he or she experiences within the group regarding radicalization and consolidation of group and collective identity; this in turn differs from what leads the terrorist to carry out acts of violence and—finally—from what leads a terrorist to become disillusioned, thus prompting him or her to leave the group.

The process of becoming a terrorist involves a cumulative, incrementally sustained, and focused commitment to the group. For the majority of contemporary terrorists—whether religious or secular—there is an early entrance onto the pathway into terrorism with many stations along the way. Also, as we have seen, there is a continuing reinforcement by manipulative leaders by consolidating the collective identity and by externalizing, justifying, and requiring violence against the enemy. This implies that early intervention is required, for once a youth is embedded within the group his or her extremist psychology is continually reinforced and any doubts diminished. Given that the attraction to, and entrance into, the terrorist path is a gradual process—which for some groups begins in early childhood—changing the influences on this pathway necessarily occur over an extended time frame. In other words, generational change is necessary, which will require a sustained effort over decades.

As important as understanding what leads youth into the path of terrorism is understanding what leads terrorists to leave—especially the processes that occur within the group or organization at this crucial juncture. Again, these will differ from group to group and from terrorist type to terrorist type. Identifying them, however, has important implications for counterterrorist policy. Indeed, John Horgan pointed out that by understanding group exit we can identify and articulate specific themes that may help to weaken the attractions of the group.[9]

Organization and Structure

Like the terrorist life cycle, organizational structure has an important impact on terrorist behavior, particularly on decision making within the group. For example, groups may adhere to the same underlying ideology but may differ remarkably in organizational structure. Thus, Hamas, Islamic Jihad, and Al-Qaeda all find justification in the Koran for killing in the name of God, but the organizational form of both Hamas and Islamic Jihad is traditionally more hierarchical and authoritarian, with followers in action cells directed from higher organizational levels to carry out an action and having only limited say in the conduct of operations.

In contrast, Al-Qaeda has a much looser organizational form with distributed decision making, reflecting the leadership style of bin Laden. The decentralization of decision making was intensified after the effective destruction of Al-Qaeda command and control in Afghanistan in 2001, leading some terrorism experts to conclude that

Al-Qaeda as it was before the U.S. attacks of September 11, 2001, is now functionally dead as an operational organization. What has been termed the *new Al-Qaeda* is considered by many to be more an ideology than an organization. The successor, the global Salafi jihad network, is widely distributed and semi-autonomous, operating more out of hubs than nodes, with wide latitude to plan and execute operations. The Madrid train bombings of March 11, 2004, reflect this emerging network.[10]

Furthermore, although most Muslim immigrants and refugees are not stateless, many suffer from an existential sense of loss, deprivation, and alienation from the countries where they live. They are often exposed to extreme ideologies that radicalize them and can foster entering the path of terrorism. The disapora has been identified as particularly important for the global Salafi jihad, with a large percentage—up to 80 percent—of recruits joining and becoming radicalized there. The London transit system bombings of July 7, 2005, can be traced to this diaspora (see Olivier Roy's and Gabriel Sheffer's contributions in this book).

Areas of Debate

Two specific areas of contemporary debate exist in which a full understanding of terrorist psychology may be of significance. The first concerns terrorists' potential use of weapons of mass destruction (WMD), such as devices involving chemical, biological, and nuclear materials. There is a broad consensus among scholars of terrorism that, for most terrorist groups, the use of such weapons would be counterproductive. Most terrorist groups seek to influence the West and to call attention to their cause; mass casualty terrorism would be contrary to their aims. It is crucial, however, to distinguish between discriminate and indiscriminate terrorism, for some terrorist groups would entertain the use of such weapons on a tactical basis if they could guaranteed they would not injure their own constituents. Furthermore, exceptions in terms of motivation are fundamentalist Islamist terrorists, especially the Salafi jihadists who are not interested in influencing the West but want to expel its corrupt modernizing values, and right-wing terrorists, who often seek revenge. For example in contrast to the Egyptian Islamic Jihad, because the Salafi jihadists are not embedded in a particular nation they are therefore particularly dangerous. It needs to be emphasized, though, that in addition to motivations and psychology, resource and expertise are required; it also can be argued that the assistance of states would be necessary for terrorist groups to produce effective WMD, especially in relation to nuclear terrorism. Without such assistance, biological terrorism is the most threatening WMD terrorism in which substate groups might become engaged.[11]

A second area of debate is the psychological effects of the new media. Identifying these effects—especially the impact of the 24/7 cable news environment and the Internet—and grappling with the approaches to countering them is a serious challenge. The new media, particularly the Internet, play an increasingly important role in establishing a sense of community among otherwise widely dispersed alienated youth. The danger in this is that the community is driven and unified by an increasingly radical anti-Western ideology. In terms of counterterrorist policy, terrorist communiqués, ideological writings, hate speech, and Internet propaganda should not go unanswered but should be responded to by well-reasoned counterargumentation.

Policy Implications

Having outlined some of the key structures and processes, it is possible to derive some policy recommendations that would enhance current efforts in the war on terrorism. This so-called war is unlike other wars, and it will require concerted efforts over decades. Just as the terrorists' collective identity has been shaped gradually over many years, the attitudes at the foundation of terrorism will not quickly be altered. When hatred has been bred in the bone—when socialization to hatred and violence begins early and is reinforced and consolidated into a major theme of the collective identity—there can be no short-term solution.

Research

Interventions designed to break this cycle must begin early—that is, before that identity is consolidated. The nature of those interventions should be informed by the systematic study of the lives of terrorists; by differentiating among terrorist types in general and groups in particular; and by understanding each terrorism in a nuanced manner within its own particular cultural, historical, and political context. Given the different demographic, pathways, attitudes, and motivations, this makes it necessary to conduct field work, including interviews with captured or defected terrorists. One cannot counter a group that one does not understand

Furthermore, if the goal of terrorism is to terrorize, terror is the property of the terrorized. Programs that reduce vulnerability to terror and promote societal resilience represent a key component of antiterrorism. Such programs require research designed to understand what steps can immunize society against terror and can promote societal resilience.

Society and Governance

As mentioned previously, it will require decades to change the culture of hatred and violence. In this struggle, the moral high ground needs to be maintained, for example by strengthening the rule of law and by exemplifying good governance and social justice. To depart from these standards is to lower ourselves to the level of the terrorists and to damage liberal democracy.

Early interventions are required to inhibit entrance onto this violent path. Such interventions should involve educational, religious, and social organization as well as the media, providing opportunities for integration and countering message of hatred against the minority. Such interventions should be based on social science research, as are the successful programs designed to curb youth gang violence.

All this highlights the fact that the struggle against terrorism is by no means a responsibility for the security services alone. This is not to say, however, that the military has no role to play in countering terrorism. The use of armed forces can be highly significant in relation to sanctuary denial: Without the existence of sanctuaries like Afghanistan, the training and planning required to support complex operations like the September 11 attacks will be extremely difficult.

Diaspora Communities

Considering the growing number of vulnerable individuals in émigré and diaspora communities, interventions that respect cultural differences while helping to integrate the refugees with the recipient society will be important. Western governments should directly support the development and implementation of community-based interventions aimed at promoting community- and individual-level changes that support greater incorporation and integration of refugees and diaspora youth into the political culture of Western liberal democracies.

Public Diplomacy and Strategic Communication

Given that terrorism is a vicious species of psychological warfare waged through the media, it cannot be countered with smart bombs and missiles: psychological warfare must be countered with psychological warfare. Each phase of the terrorist life cycle is a potential focus of intervention. In other words, counterterrorist measures must be designed to:

- Inhibit potential terrorists from joining the group. Once inside the group, the power of group dynamics is immense, continually confirming the power of the group's organizing ideology and reinforcing the member's dedication to the cause.

- Produce dissension in the group.
- Facilitate exit from the group. It is important to stimulate and encourage defection from the group. A number of states with significant terrorism problems—Italy, Spain in the Basque region, and Great Britain in Northern Ireland—have creatively employed amnesty programs to facilitate terrorists leaving the group.
- Reduce support for the group and its leader. If for every terrorist killed or captured, ten more are waiting in line, it is critical to marginalize the group and to deromanticize and delegitimate the leader. In the case of radical Islamist terrorism, this can only be done from within Islam, with moderate Arab political leaders and moderate Muslim clerics taking on the extremists in their midst who have hijacked their nations and their religion. The goal is to alienate the terrorist organization from its constituency, which plays a crucial role in providing a reservoir of new recruits. This, in turn, will inhibit potential terrorists from joining the group or organization in the first place. [12]

However, all these measures—however much needed—assume an understanding of the significance of psychological dynamics on the behavior of individual terrorists or terrorist groups. Unfortunately, in many cases, counterterrorist policies demonstrate no such awareness, and the first challenge therefore lies in increasing the knowledge and consciousness of these mechanism and dynamics among officials and decision makers.

Endnotes

1. This essay is based on a chapter titled "The Mind of the Terrorist," in Post, *Leaders and Their Followers in a Dangerous World* (Ithaca, NY: Cornell University Press, 2004) [Chapter 6, pg. 123-161]. It also draws on the final paper of recommendations released by the Psychology Working Group, International Summit on Democracy, Terrorism and Security, Madrid, March 2005, http://www.clubmadrid.org.
2. See Post, "Notes on a Psychodynamic Theory of Terrorism," *Terrorism* 3 (1984) [pg. 241-256].
3. This summary is drawn from Post, "Mind of the Terrorist."
4. Post, Ehud Sprinzak, and Laurita M. Denny, "Terrorists in Their Own Words: Interviews with 35 Incarcerated Middle Eastern Terrorists," *Terrorism and Political Violence* 15, no. 1 (2003) [pg. 177].

5. See Eric Hoffer, The True Believer: *Thoughts on the Nature of Mass Movements* (New York: Harper, 1951).
6. Hafez, Muhammed Manufacturing Human Bombs, US Institute of Peace (in press).
7. Ariel Merari, personal communication with author, Fall 2003.
8. Dean A. Minix and Andrew Semmel, "Group Dynamics and Risk-Taking: An Experimental Examination," *Experimental Study of Politics* 6, no. 3 (1978) [pg. 1-36].
9. John Horgan, "Disengaging," in *The Psychology of Terrorism*, ed. Horgan (New York: Routledge, 2005) [pg. 140-168].
10. For the idea of netwar, see John Arquilla, David Ronfeldt, and Michele Zanini, "Networks, Netwar, and Information-Age Terrorism," in *Countering the New Terrorism*, ed. Ian O. Lesser and others (Washington, DC: RAND, 1999) [pg. 45-56].
11. See Post, "Psychological and Motivational Factors in Terrorist Decision-Making: Implications for CBW Terrorism," in *Toxic Terror: Assessing Terrorist Use of Chemical and Biological Weapons*, ed. Jonathan B. Tucker (Cambridge, MA: MIT Press, 2000) [pg. 11-12].
12. For an extended discussion of the role of psychological operations in countering terrorism, see Post, J. "Psychological Operations and Counter-terrorism," *Joint Force Quarterly*, Spring 2005.

3

Suicide Terrorism

Nasra Hassan

"Preparing and carrying out a suicide operation is neither difficult nor expensive," I hear repeatedly during my research on Islamist militancy. "However, the recipe must not be used carelessly, but only for maximum impact, or when other avenues are not available." A suicide bombing is never a spontaneous act by an individual; instead, it is the result of planning and execution by a sponsoring group. It has become terrorists' preferred method, because a determined suicide bomber has a better chance than other operatives of reaching the target, and the psychological trauma inflicted by a suicide operation increases the impact and raises the profile of its sponsors in addition to causing death and injury.

My interest in human bombs started in the 1990s, when I worked and lived in the Middle East. As a Muslim woman from Pakistan, I could not comprehend how and why people blow themselves up in the name of a higher cause, whether it be Islam or the homeland. My research, which continues, has yielded a data bank of over 300 profiles of Palestinian, other Arab, Pakistani, Afghan, Kashmiri, and Bangladeshi suicide bombers and their sponsors. The profiles are based on detailed information from families, friends, sponsoring groups, militants, jihadis, and security officials, as well as from documents given to me. In some cases, however, the information is sketchy.[1]

Very useful material has emerged from interviews—conducted over many years—with leaders, planners, and trainers of groups that sponsor suicide operations. In my research I also document the adoption and adaptation of suicide tactics and evolution in the types of groups and individuals involved. In this chapter, I focus on Pakistani suicide squads because relatively little is known about them. Most suicide operations in the Islamic world differ only slightly from a blueprint which contains a set of essentials that is then adapted to the respective local circumstances. First, I outline this blueprint, then provide an overview of my findings in the case of Pakistan, and finally compare the Pakistani case to suicide operations sponsored by Palestinian groups.

The Blueprint

The timing and decision to include suicide bombings in the arsenal of resistance operations usually result from a considered agreement at the highest levels of a militant group. It is often initiated by the impassioned plea of supporters who point to its success elsewhere. After the start of the first Palestinian Intifada (uprising) in December 1987, for example, it took six years and a long internal debate before the strategy was adopted, following a great deal of discussion among the leaderships in the Gaza Strip, the West Bank, and the Palestinian diaspora. On the other hand, a jihadi leader told me that the decision to launch suicide operations in Afghanistan and Pakistan was taken at a single meeting in Karachi in November 2001, six weeks after the start of the post-September 11, 2001, bombing of Afghanistan.

Religion-based sponsoring groups say that the intention in carrying out a suicide operation is important: The act must be for Allah alone—never for personal gain. Whereas nationalist groups refer to freedom and fighting occupation, many Palestinian and Iraqi nationalists used Islamic terminology in their last will and testament. Hamas, Palestinian Islamic Jihad, and Al-Qaeda affiliates in the Middle East have begun to insert homeland reasons in theirs. Suicide jihadis in Pakistan and, increasingly, in Iraq set their reasoning in sectarian terms and in the wider context of the Muslim *ummah* (nation).

Irrespective of the use of religious rhetoric, which generally should not be dismissed, suicide attacks are considered military operations by their sponsors. As such, they are driven by military-type considerations, as are operations by other nonstate and substate actors such as insurgents, guerrillas, and rebels. Factors enabling the adoption of, and support for, suicide operations are causes and grievances that deeply and emotionally affect the world of Islam and Muslims—even the secular ones. Such issues are generally clear cut between Muslim and non-Muslim and have an undeniable resonance and consensus, regardless of religiosity, nationalist fervor, upbringing, or social background. The resonance ensures not only a ready supply of suicide operators but also vocal or silent support from communities that may otherwise oppose attacks whose victims are mainly Muslim.

A charismatic figure is a key ingredient in inspiring martyrdom (see Jerrold Post's contribution in this book), whereas television and the Internet bring distant causes into real time and immediacy. *Fatwas* (religious edicts) give legitimacy, but the "okay to do" edicts are taken more seriously than the "don't do" ones, especially since the former outrank and outnumber the latter, appear to have weightier religious sanction and find greater resonance. The edicts that prohibit are too cautiously worded to have the same impact and often contain too many exclusionary clauses to have much effect. The *fatwa* issued in May 2005 by fifty-eight Pakistani clerics from major schools of Islamic thought banned suicide bombings in Pakistan and Kashmir and in places of worship and where the victims are likely to be Muslims; Iraq and Palestine were excluded from the ban. A counter-fatwa by forty religious parties permitted suicide attacks in Palestine, Kashmir, Iraq and Afghanistan, but not in Pakistan.

Sponsoring groups are helped by neural pathways, which connect networks of families, clans, tribes, and friends. The more extremist militants are, the more likely they are to marry into a family that shares their views; in some cases, marriage into an extremist family increases their militancy. For example, the sister of a major militant in the Balochistan province of Pakistan is married to Ramzi Yusuf, who is serving a life sentence in the United States for plotting the 1993 Twin Towers bombing in New York City. The sympathizers of suicide terrorism, on the other hand, are a mix of pious Muslims, supporters of jihad, fanatics, militants, and sectarian haters. Defense of Islam and of Muslims—as defined by them—is the political ideology and justification for suicide and related terrorism by the groups, operators, and supporters. Clandestine support from official structures is often available, either as an officially sanctioned but deniable rogue operation or as silent policy.

The targets are, first and foremost, enemy structures and authorities: their own, if considered un-Islamic or tyrannical; or external ones such as occupation troops, external or internal allies of the enemy (the latter represented by the army, police, or civilian officials), and sectarian or ideological enemies. "It is not our intention to kill innocent civilians, but we are in a state of war," the jihadis have told me. "And the majority of civilians killed by the enemy are Muslims." Lists are drawn up of optimal targets, locations, and timing. The go-ahead is based on opportunity and feasibility, and the funds required are minimal.

The objectives are many. In addition to wreaking loss, destruction, and havoc, suicide operations carry actual and symbolic messages for different audiences: the world at large, enemy governments and peoples, the Islamic world, and their own comrades. Other than revenge and retaliation—measured by the actual devastation caused—suicide attacks contain an explicit or implicit warning to potential targets. They are a show of defiance and strength on the jihadi battlefield. "Sometimes we send a suicide bomber even if we could use a timer or remote detonator," a Palestinian planner told me in the Gaza Strip. "The human element creates much more panic among the people, which is an important military goal in itself."

Importantly, the sponsors gauge the fallout, especially among those who support their cause or are neutral on the issue. "We value life, which is why we are willing to face death. Since Paradise awaits the martyr, exchanging a temporary life for an immortal one is a good bargain," I have been told. The reaction of Muslims is an important consideration in the decision-making process, as is the inevitable reprisal. "Our operation is a balm for the aching hearts of our *ummah* and brings them some relief," I have heard. Unlike the public manifestation of joy at the attacks on the U.S. on September 11, 2001, the reaction to the July 7, 2005, bombings in London was deliberately muted. "We were expecting something to happen, so when it did, we did not clap and dance, especially for television, as we did in September 2001. But we felt a great satisfaction, since far more oppression has been visited on the *ummah* everywhere after 9/11 than deaths caused by Muslims," a Pakistani jihadi leader told me in summer 2005.

Suicide Operations in Pakistan

Although Pakistanis are relative newcomers to suicide terrorism involving explosives, they have quickly become adept at it. Terrorism in Pakistan is polygonal, with each side of a loose structure fitting into a template belonging to another set-up, whether religious extremist, sectarian, nationalist, criminal, or mercenary. The suicide squads display a wide range of ideologies and motivations. They mutate rapidly, hide inside other groups, disappear, dissolve, and reappear. Sometimes members of different groups carry out an operation under a name not belonging to an established entity. Indeed, it is difficult to track down a ghost group, as the experience of Lebanon in the 1980s demonstrates. Their targets are multiple, and their wings and cells are led by an inordinately large number of young, educated, middle-class professionals who have little reason to be alienated or enraged to the extent of adopting suicide terrorism as a profession.

The origins of Pakistan's suicide terrorism lie in a sectarian jihad: against fellow Muslims, the Shias. It has been waged by Lashkar e Jhangvi (LeJ), a militant Sunni organization that has attracted to its ranks the most extreme elements from other jihadi groups. Prior to September 11, 2001, LeJ used the elasticity and osmosis afforded by cross-membership in groups associated with Al-Qaeda and the Taliban to find an early foothold in Afghanistan. Since then, it has reinvented itself as the purveyor of suicide terrorism in Pakistan. Despite LeJ's sui generis character, its hybrid aspects and mutation offer a useful comparison with terrorist groupings and their modus operandi elsewhere in the Islamic world—in particular in Iraq—and to Islamist militants in the West.

In late 1999, jihadi groups introduced suicide attacks in Kashmir, with young men detonating themselves against enemy targets. After the post 9/11 bombing of Afghanistan and the fall of the Taliban regime, this modus operandi began to find favor in an environment of humiliation and resulting rage, encouraged in sermons by Arab militants fleeing from Afghanistan, in endorsement by Pakistani clerics, and in immediate acceptance by hardened jihadi cadres who were familiar with traditional martyrdom operations in which survival was a priori ruled out. As of end-December 2005, 139 Muslim human bombers had blown themselves up in 115 suicide operations in Pakistan, Kashmir, India, Afghanistan, and Bangladesh.

The methodology of Lashkar e Jhangvi and its associated cadres underwent an evolution, becoming more sophisticated. Starting with an individual human bomb carrying explosives, the suicide squads graduated to the use of explosives-laden vehicles and then to complex attacks in which they use, in sequence: (1) hand grenades to create panic and to kill; (2) gunfire to block escape and to kill; (3) time bombs to create additional victims among those who rush to the scene for rescue work; and, finally, (4) the self-detonation of the two- or three-member team. Sometimes the sequence in the detonation of time bombs and human bombs is reversed. The plastic explosives used are powerful enough to split open a cupola roof and to fling body parts twenty meters into the air. Despite official attempts to ascribe foreign origins to them, the vast majority of the suicide bombers were locals. Half the suicide attacks have been in or near a place of worship, and creating fear and terror is as much part of the operation as is death and destruction. If the primary target is inaccessible, a proxy target is selected—for example, Christian victims in churches and schools, if Western officials are too well protected.

Pakistan's sprawling jihadi networks are based on national, regional, and international contacts, cooperation, and operations.

The groups work closely with each other. Cooperation takes many forms, from a loan or barter of militants, expertise, supplies, and funds to an alliance or friendly exchange of causes and targets. Members from different groups come together for a suicide operation or cross over from a defunct group into an active one. This constant movement makes it difficult for the authorities to trace the real sponsors. Lashkar's ranks are swollen with militants who are overtly affiliated with other jihadi groups such as Jaish e Mohammad but who secretly retain membership in LeJ. Many start out as nonmilitants who, after being brutalized in prison, join LeJ following escape or release. To survive, they become underground killers, as normal life and a fair judicial process are a distant dream. It is almost impossible to separate junior-level jihadi extremists from different groups; they only assume a distinct identity when they reach senior positions.

The link among militancy, madrassas, and jihad is the subject of much attention. My research shows that madrassas and mosque schools are not the major producer and vector of suicide jihadis. Since the emphasis of the curricula is on Islam, jihad and martyrdom are naturally favored subjects, and some students go on to adopt jihad as a vocation, part- or full-time profession, or mission. A suction system attracts future operators not only from the large reservoir of sympathizers found all over the country but also from secular state and private schools; universities; professional institutions; the business, trade, and bazaar sectors; as well as from government ranks, including the armed forces. Prior to September 11, 2001, camps inside Pakistan provided training mainly for action in Kashmir. Afghan jihadis and their Pakistani, Arab, and Central Asian comrades essentially learned on the job in Afghanistan or received rudimentary lessons in the refugee camps in Pakistan. Novices were assigned to veteran groups and either learned quickly or were killed. Many were autodidacts. Training camps and the jihad in Afghanistan brought Pakistani militants into a network, which has grown tighter as traditional safe havens have disappeared.

The jihadis I have interviewed in Pakistan since 1998 told me about their most potent weapon: the squads of martyr commandos, who received martyrdom training in special camps. They were eighteen to thirty years old; most were middle or lower middle class, although some were the sons of rich men and even government officials. About half were married. The majority were students who enrolled for jihad training and fought during vacations; the rest had jobs, some in lower-government echelons.

R. was a typical jihadi militant I met in an industrial town in the Punjab. He graduated from a training camp with distinction.

With skills honed on the battlefield, he became a part-time recruiter, fundraiser and trainer—in between taking turns with his brothers in running the large family business. He described to me the training, which was based on a percolation system. The twenty-one-day basic training class contained about twenty youths; the boys were taught to clean and to assemble light weapons and received lessons on Islam, jihad, and Paradise. Three-quarters of the spiritual training took place in this initial period. About eight boys made it into the three-month training and five into the nine-month training, and maybe two graduated from the two-year training course. "Those who graduated after two years were explosives experts and were the most valuable. Although it is a waste of investment, the best of the best go for suicide attacks, because it has become exceedingly difficult to pull off any other kind of major operation, except a final mission. Only the best have the iron resolve to complete it," R. told me.

The training covered weaponry, including small missiles; underwater skills; motorbike stunts such as firing with both hands while driving; trapping and attacking larger, better-armed military units; and practicing ambushing and hijacking with elaborate mock-ups. And students were trained to martyr themselves or to be martyred while inflicting maximum loss. Like their Muslim counterparts elsewhere, the trainees, all of whom had code names, made regular ablutions to be in a constant state of purity for sudden entry into Paradise.

K., a graduate from an English language school in Lahore with a Western curriculum and who became a writer and journalist, described for me a typical day at his camp. "We woke up two hours before sunrise for prayers and spiritual exercises. We prayed five times a day. Twice a day we heard lectures on jihad by mullah commandos, who drew lessons from the Quran and the sayings of the Prophet Muhammad and told us of the forty grades of martyrdom. During the two daily breaks, we listened to tapes of jihad chants and sermons." Those in the martyr squads prepared a last will and testament using special texts. Occasionally, famous jihad veterans visited from across the border to train, to inspire, and to select commandos.

The number of martyrdom trainees normally did not exceed 50 at any given point, with 100 an exceptional peak. The numbers were replenished as the need arose, with *need* often being related to government liquidation. "This does not mean that there will be 50 or 100 suicide operations," I was told. "Maybe up to 5 in a year, based on an assessment of requirement and feasibility. It means that at any given time 50 or 100 are ready to die." While they are waiting to be summoned, the martyr-commandos are ordered to live normally and to do nothing to attract attention. They are advised to take off their beards; to switch from traditional clothing to pants and shirts; to maintain a neat, everyday appearance; to avoid their usual hang-outs; and to carry documents—real ones issued to fake names—at all times. They are forbidden even to run a red light and are told to pay their bills on time and to do nothing out of the ordinary.

However, in my research I also encountered cases of suicide bombers who had only a week between their recruitment, training, and detonation. When Lashkar e Jhangvi's operational structure was still centralized, before the arrest and liquidation of its leaders, its cells were small—between three and five members each. Later, having had to assume greater decentralized responsibility, the cells became larger and all-purpose. They now disband after each operation and regroup for the next one. Traditionally, the key components of a cell are (1) the leader, (2) the suicide bomber and suicide gunman, and (3) the linkman in charge of logistics, communications, and arrange-ments. With decentralized networks and cells, linkmen are the most critical field operatives and are the bridge between sponsors and the cell leaders. They transmit instructions and funds, organize the raw materials, arrange for the explosives, advise among options, and con-vey the go-ahead. Seasoned linkmen are considered a jihadi group's most important resource, as they usually initiate the establishment of multiple cells unconnected to each other for simultaneous, consecu-tive, or delayed use. They are not in the most senior echelons of the group and often play a similar role in more than one jihadi outfit.

At present, most cells need to be capable of providing one-stop services. They are stand alone structures in terms of on-the-ground planning, reconnaissance, and execution of a suicide attack. In view of the Pakistani government's counterterrorism efforts, the cells are encouraged to self-finance, which they increasingly do through armed robbery and kidnappings. The commands, which emanate from a higher level of the organization, relay the timing, target, and location of a suicide operation. These are based on a set of factors, such as the immediate reason for a suicide operation, location of the nearest bomber, ease of access to the target, and whether the sponsors can afford yet another severe crackdown by the authorities. LeJ recruits hitmen and operatives with care, looking for strong conviction and steady nerves. In the beginning, a novice is paired with a veteran and drives the motorbike while the assassin takes out the target. An LeJ trainee code-named "Ghaddafi" lost his nerve and was captured by the police. On his way to liquidation, he asked why he was being removed from his cell at midnight. "We are putting you on the fast train to Paradise," he was told, echoing an extremist slogan: Kill a shia, and go to Paradise. As a warning, his body was dumped in the militants' belt in the southern Punjab.

The selection of the suicide team and the availability of suicide bombers do not pose a serious problem. Since supply continues to exceed demand, the cell leader considers only men who are ready to go. Depending on the specifics of the planned operation, the wing or cell leader sifts out volunteers considered unsuitable or not yet prepared, refuses to accept highly trained cadres whose expertise—for example, in explosives—is indispensable for the group, places the names of suitable and ready candidates in a box, and pulls out five or six names. Two are the suicide bombers, one is a gunman who will also die, and two are back-ups. Once a suicide team is ready, it is considered necessary to dispatch them sooner rather than later. "Young suicide bombers don't have a long shelf life, and the cell leader also blows himself up in a future operation, since his capture is only a question of time," an LeJ militant told me.

The leadership is careful not to select many attackers from the same community, since too many losses and too tough a crackdown by the authorities would provoke too furious a backlash against the jihadi group. "A measured suicide operation and a response within expected parameters fills our ranks," an experienced jihadi told me. "This is not child's play. We must consider our tactics within the group's long-term strategy. We know the level of losses we can afford, but too much would be counterproductive in the longer term."

When two suicide operations are scheduled to take place in the same town, the cell leaders bring in bombers from different areas, preferably distant ones. The suicide candidates are generally not fugitives, though some may have been detained in an arrest campaign or in connection with petty crime. It is preferred that they not be wanted by the authorities or known LeJ militants with a price on their heads. In contrast, cell and wing leaders—by virtue of years spent in operations—are on official wanted lists and carry large bounties for information leading to their capture. Cell operations have acquired an assembly-line character, different from the theatrical productions of earlier times when militants watched Hollywood films for ideas on stunts and scenarios. In its heyday, Lashkar e Jhangvi's commander in chief, Riaz Basra, ran an elaborate system of area chiefs, who were responsible for recruitment; coordination; identification and reconnaissance of targets; logistics; execution of operations; intimidation of officials, judges, lawyers, and witnesses, for which there was a special section; infiltration into lower-government echelons; and a media and information wing. Financing came from donations based on conviction or coercion and from charity and alms mandated by Islam.

The families of martyred militants received a monthly stipend. The highest amount was set aside to purchase weapons, explosives, and unlisted telephone numbers of officials who were targeted for assassination or intimidation. There is no organized communal postmartyrdom industry to glorify suicide bombers: They are commemorated within the organization but not in the community at large. When, where, and how a suicide operation can be mounted determine its execution. However, where the exact timing is not dependent on the agenda and movement of the target, LeJ prefers to time a suicide operation to catch the evening news and the press deadline. A militant often dictates details to a newspaper reporter on the phone; if the event goes unpublished, a threatening call is made to find out why the item was not released.

Four factors complicate the task of isolating the DNA of Pakistani suicide operatives—that is, special characteristics that might set them apart from thousands of other jihadis and militants:

Individually, their roots in Pakistan's provincial, ethnic, sectarian, class, and cultural divides—that is, their very ordinariness and similarity to millions of Pakistani males.

Organizationally, their sequential or simultaneous membership in multiple groups and their deliberate interchangeability.

Ideologically, their mutation from sectarian zealots to cross-border jihadis.

The dynamics of shifting motivations and motives for suicide operations.

The following typology of Pakistani suicide bombers and volunteers developed from my research shows that, similar to suicide bombers elsewhere, there is no single profile or mind of the terrorist and that their characteristics match those of the general population.

1. Age: The majority of the suicide bombers were between eighteen and thirty; the volunteers were all in their mid- and late thirties.

2. Education: Less than half had attended madrassas or mosque schools, especially if no other schooling was available; the rest went to government schools, and half had higher schooling, including university.

3. Socioeconomic situation: 50 percent were middle or lower-middle class, 30 percent were upper class or rich, and 20 percent were poor.

4. Marital status: The majority of suicide bombers were single; of the volunteers, about half were married.
5. Family and community: Normal in the local context.
6. Family militancy: About one-third belonged to jihad-affiliated families.
7. Personality: Almost all were described as courageous, resolute, and serious with no evidence of brainwashing, coercion, or psychological problems.
8. Religious practice: About one-third were described as very religious; the rest observed obligatory practices only.
9. Intention: Only for a higher cause, never for personal gain.
10. Paradise as motivation: Less than 20 percent cited this.
11. Importance of martyrdom: All referred to this.
12. Mosque affiliation: The majority did not pray regularly in a mosque.
13. Charismatic influence: Well-known cleric leaders, especially those who had engaged in jihad (dissemination via speeches, sermons, and cassettes), imams, jihadi heroes.
14. Hero: Osama bin Laden cited by all.
15. Enabling factors: Causes and grievances that deeply and emotionally affected the bombers and their communities, or were presented as such by the sponsors.
16. Resonating factors in decision to volunteer for suicide operation: Defense of Islam, retaliation for betrayal of Al-Qaeda and Taliban, revenge on authorities for bowing to external pressure, sectarian issues, ratcheted-up need and desire for retaliation. The resonance not only ensures a ready supply of suicide bomber recruits but also swells the ranks of the sponsoring group and creates support in the community.
17. No special resonance: For example, Palestine, Jerusalem, Iraq, and Chechnya not cited.
18. Training: The majority of the suicide bombers had received training in special camps or had fought in either Afghanistan or Kashmir or both; almost all the volunteers were repeat jihadis; that is, they had returned to militancy after a period of dormancy.
19. Work: The majority were gainfully employed or had a source of income, except those who were students or underground.

Pakistani Suicide Bombers in Comparison

Although two sets of profiles I have developed—of Palestinian and Pakistani suicide bombers and their sponsoring groups—are unequal in numbers, some characteristics of the Pakistani suicide bombers match their counterparts from Hamas and Palestinian Islamic Jihad, and other traits match those of suicide bombers from the al Aqsa Martyrs Brigade and the Popular Front for the Liberation of Palestine (PFLP).

General similarities in the environment that have an impact on the individual include the Islamic religion and culture; a premium on martyrdom; deliberate retention and cultivation of memory, passed down and resurrected in each new generation of recruits; breakdown in law and order; a charismatic figure in the immediate environment of the individual; a history of jihad or resistance or both; presence of sponsoring groups and ready-made networks that encourage, enable, and ennoble suicide operations; ease of joining the groups at the periphery and traveling the jihadi path toward a progressively final destination; a tight and strong group culture, rituals, language, and lifestyle; a neuralgic point when suicide terrorism is introduced and is enthusiastically accepted and adopted; and easy availability of volunteers, with supply exceeding demand. Poverty, dislocation, and psychopathology were not found to be causal factors in creating suicide terrorists.

At the individual level, the similarity relates to there being no set psychological, social, or militant type, per se. In both sets, there is strong anecdotal evidence of potent feelings of humiliation and rage, of a strong desire to do something about the actual or perceived grievances of their group or *ummah,* of membership in a group, and of lack of confidence in authorities and the judicial system. The individuals in each set were described as serious, quiet, determined, committed, generous, helpful, and kind. Although not explicitly voiced, evidence exists of a desire to overcome the passive victim role by assuming a proactive one: We will die anyway, so why not go in a noble manner at a time of our choosing? There is a clear understanding of the finality and consequences of the contemplated act; one Pakistani militant interviewed stated that he wished to explode only against a really important target.

There are also general differences in the environment. In Pakistan, there is no clear conflation of religion and nationalism in suicide terrorism—for example, a double suicide bombing targeted President Pervez Musharraf in December 2003 for his pro-U.S. and anti-Al-Qaeda and Taliban stand; no foreign occupation or troops; easy access to explosives and expertise and freedom to move, hide, and melt away; and, so far, no purely nationalist insurgent group involved in suicide bombings.

A number of ongoing armed insurgencies and conflicts muddy the picture versus a clear Palestinian–Israeli issue. In Pakistan, few robust and sustained voices are raised on the unlawfulness of suicide attacks. Some who oppose these inside Pakistan favor them in Kashmir, Iraq, and in the Palestinian territories—wherever non-Muslim authorities are present in superior strength. Despite the harrowing 1947 partition of British India into two independent states—India and Pakistan—and the resulting forced or voluntary movement of persons across borders, there is no systematic inherited communal cultivation of the national memory of lost rights and homes, except in the case of Kashmir. A major reason for this is that, unlike the case of the Palestinians, there were no continuing generations of officially recognized refugees after the displaced acquired an accepted homeland.

At the individual level, the Pakistani suicide operators were older and less articulate, displayed a less defined purpose and a less coherent worldview; used less political and more religious and sectarian arguments, had a less developed and less enunciated language of Paradise and martyrdom that stemmed from lack of knowledge of religious texts, and possessed a strong sectarian but no nationalist flavor. Membership in the most extremist and militant group, Lashkar e Jhangvi, was important for them. Postmartyrdom glory and glorification of suicide martyrs is not a developed industry in Pakistan, and the Palestinians leave behind much more materials and memories—oral, written, pictorial, and legendary—than do the Pakistanis.

* * * * *

The internal and external evolution in the sponsoring groups and in the profiles of its suicide squads continue, as do the expansion and adaptation of suicide terrorism. No sooner do researchers and terrorism experts begin to consolidate their findings than new manifestations and forms emerge. The latter do not necessarily negate the earlier findings but instead demonstrate that the phenomenon of suicide terrorism is not receding and has not yet been fully understood. We still cannot properly explain, for example, unexpected targeted locations (e.g., London), home-grown Western suicide bombers, active but clandestine recruitment at universities and among middle-class professionals, and the rapid mutations in terrorism. One thing, though, is for certain: as one LeJ militant—who has since been liquidated—told me in 2003, "Our operations are never random. We have no problem with shedding the blood of those whom it is a duty to kill."

Endnotes

1. All interviewees provided information on condition of strict ano-
   nymity, covering up names, locations, dates, or other references
   which could identify them. This was done both for their protection
   and for my own. The material in this chapter was taken from my
   unpublished book on Muslim suicide bombers, as well as from an
   unpublished study of Lashkar e Jhangvi.

Political Roots

4

Democracy and Terrorism

Leonard Weinberg

Repression works: Brutal dictatorships rarely suffer campaigns of terrorist violence—at least not for very long. In the Middle East the record
seems clear. When challenged by religiously inspired terrorist bands in
the 1980s, the Baathist regimes of Syria and of Iraq under Saddam Hussein employed the tools of their trade (e.g., secret police surveillance,
mass arrests, torture, summary executions) and brought these challenges to a speedy conclusion. The same may be said about the conduct
of the revolutionary theocracy in Iran. In 1980–81 the anti-Khomeini
Mujaheddin and Fedayeen launched a particularly ferocious terrorist
campaign aimed at toppling the new government in Tehran, including
the assassination of the country's newly elected president. In response
the government unleashed the revolutionary guards and other forces
and managed to bring an end to the violence, along with many of its
perpetrators, within a few months. Over the years, the few democracies
in the region—Turkey, Israel, and Lebanon—have been much less successful. In fact, as recent events in New York City, Madrid, and London
suggest, terrorism seems largely, though not exclusively, a problem for
democracies. I intend the following comments to answer two questions:
First, what are the sources of terrorism within democracies? Second,
why are democracies, or at least some of them, targeted for attack by
international terrorist organizations?

Sources of Terrorism in Democracies

Thinking about terrorism's domestic political causes, the highly regarded analyst Martha Crenshaw[1] suggests we distinguish between permissive or facilitating causes and direct or instigating factors and also among the sources of terrorism within democracies. Identifying these causes is obviously no easy task, but it nevertheless offers an easy way out: We may be tempted to generalize so broadly that we speak only platitudes. I may not be able to avoid this pitfall but will at least try.

Two problems stand out when we consider permissive conditions making for terrorism within democracies. First, what appear to be the same political conditions may give rise to terrorism in one place or at one time but not another. During the late 1960s mass student protests against the Vietnam War and the repressive atmosphere and overcrowded classrooms of universities gave rise to widespread terrorist activity in Italy but not in France. A second problem is that thanks to the mass media, the Internet, and other means by which behavior can be diffused and copied, terrorist campaigns within democracies may spread from one country to another even though political conditions within those countries differ significantly. As a consequence, the predictive capacity of background conditions is now limited. We may observe little beyond certain tendencies. Despite these difficulties, a number of permissive conditions receive considerable commentary in the literature, categorized as either (1) temporal conditions or (2) structural elements. Tore Bjorgo and others suggest that transitional democracies or countries in which such transitions are being attempted are substantially more susceptible than long-standing democracies to outbreaks of terrorist violence, especially where the rules of the game are not clear or—as in some cases—are not accepted by the various players.[2]

Certain ethnic groups, for example, may not accept the fact that they belong to the political community undergoing the transition. If group members participate fully in and identify themselves with the old order they may want out of the new order because their leaders believe they are likely to suffer a diminution of power and status. For such groups acts of terrorism may signal their desire to exit the system or may serve as symptoms of their refusal to settle for less. Transitional democracies often face the problem of holdovers from a previous authoritarian regime; some holdovers are prepared to use terrorist violence to make the transition process as difficult as possible—for example, the Sunni minority in Iraq at the time of this writing. Even Spain experienced such terrorism during its own highly successful transition following the death of Francisco Franco.

Other research suggests that long-standing, or consolidated, democracies are about as susceptible to terrorism as new ones.[3] India, with a practically uninterrupted democratic experience since its achievement of national independence in 1947, has experienced terrorist activity over much of this history. Likewise, despite decades of uninterrupted democratic rule, Colombia continues to suffer bouts of terrorism from both the left and the right. Jan Oskar Engene's analysis of terrorist events in Western Europe identifies the United Kingdom—surely one of the world's premier examples of democratic continuity—as that region's most frequent site of internal terrorist violence from 1950 to 1995.[4]

If terrorism is present at the creation of democratic polities, it sometimes occurs at and contributes to their collapse as well. In some instances terrorist violence is directly related to the end of democracy. In the 1970s democratically elected governments in both Argentina and Uruguay were victims of military coups as a result of their apparent inability to defeat the challenges posed by various urban guerrilla groups. The military's seizure of power in Turkey at the end of the 1970s provides another example. Even though new and long-standing democracies may experience some variation in the numerical frequency of terrorist events, overall it seems fair to say that longevity by no means insulates democracies from outbreaks of internally driven terrorism.

If the duration of democracies is not the most powerful permissive condition, or of only limited explanatory power, what about the structure of democratic polities? Do variations in structure matter? If so, how great a difference do they make? Engene used his *Terrorism in Western Europe,* event data database, which covers domestic terrorist events in Western European democracies between 1950 and 1995, to consider a number of possibilities, both societal and governmental. Engene reported modest but meaningful statistical associations between ethnic diversity and the incidence of terrorist violence. The more ethnically diverse the country, the more terrorism it experiences, especially when the violence is motivated by ethnic grievances.[5] Given the majority principle, democracies that include permanent ethnic minorities are especially vulnerable. Socially homogeneous countries are much less vulnerable: Scandinavian countries show very low frequencies. The inclusion of Norway, Denmark, Sweden, and Iceland in Engene's analysis also helps to explain another linkage: income distribution. The more unevenly distributed the income, the greater is the frequency of terrorist events, especially when perpetrated by ideologically motivated groups.

Certain features of a country's political system make a difference in the frequency of terrorist events. In Engene's study, democracies with better records in protecting civil rights and civil liberties
were somewhat less likely to experience a high frequency of terrorist
attacks.[6] The problem with this finding concerns causality. It may
very well be the case that sustained terrorist attacks caused democratic governments to reduce the privacy and due process rights of
their citizens rather than these restrictions causing the terrorism.
Certainly this pattern was at work in Italy and the United Kingdom
during the 1970s as both governments grappled with serious challenges posed by terrorist or paramilitary organizations.

Engene makes a more compelling case for the impacts of legitimacy and continuity on the frequency of terrorist events. Western
European democracies, where extremist political parties—which did
not accept the prevailing constitutional order—had done well at the
polls and been a significant presence in their respective parliaments,
also suffered more terrorist violence. The same holds true for countries whose twentieth-century histories have been marked by serious
discontinuities: Germany, Italy, and Spain, by contrast with Luxembourg and the Scandinavian democracies. In short, Western European countries where Engene found terrorism to be most prevalent
tended to be noisy and highly contentious democracies.[7] In a comparative analysis of terrorism and party politics, William Eubank and
I reported analogous findings. In Europe as well as Latin America,
South Asia, and elsewhere, where multiple political parties achieved
parliamentary representation and where parliaments displayed substantial partisan divisions, democracies were more likely to experience serious terrorism than other democracies.[8] The underlying conditions seemed to be extreme social and political fragmentation.

Associations among various permissive conditions mentioned in
the literature, though statistically significant, are rarely very strong,
which should lead us to pay particularly close attention to what Martha Crenshaw identified as the direct, instigating conditions that trig-
ger terrorist campaigns. In the case of the Israeli–Palestinian struggle, certain conditions (e.g., the Israeli occupation of the West Bank
and Gaza Strip) were present for years before the outbreak of the
first Intifada in 1988. At first, the Intifada was not characterized by
much terrorist activity. The first suicide bombing, for example, only
occurred in 1993. Rather, the Israeli authorities confronted a relatively spontaneous series of violent protests involving rocks, Molotov
cocktails, and burning tires.[9] Some time elapsed before the Palestine Liberation Organization (PLO), headquartered in Tunis, and the
new Palestinian organizations Hamas and Islamic Jihad were able to

transform the conflict into a terrorist campaign. And of course in this endeavor they achieved the unintentional cooperation of the Israeli authorities who responded to their challenge with moderate brutality and mass arrests, enough to inflame the protestors but not enough to stop their protests. Periods of confinement in Israeli jails had the effect of producing a new generation of Palestinian terrorists.

What lessons can we derive from this tale? Is it a parable from which general principles can be learned and applied elsewhere? Though the Israeli–Palestinian conflict may be sui generis in some respects, the answer to this question is yes, because we see in it three instigating conditions also found elsewhere. First, the immediate condition is one of radicalization. Social and political events occur that crystallize long-standing grievances. "Attention must be paid," to quote Arthur Miller's *Death of a Salesman*. The 1968 Catholic civil rights marches in Northern Ireland might also serve as an example. Second, an occasion then arises for small entrepreneurial bands whose repertoire of political actions includes terrorism. Third, whether, or the extent to which, this opportunity is characterized by a sustained campaign of terrorism either against the government or other segments in the population—for example, rival ethnic or ideological groups—most likely depends on the behavior of the authorities.

In democracies at least, repression—as in the case of Russian conduct in Chechnya—has often produced Beslan or its equivalent. This can be compared to when India's government inadvertently sparked Sikh terrorism in the Punjab by its invasion of the Golden Temple. Also of note, Timothy McVeigh's detonation of a truck bomb in front of the Murrah Federal Building in Oklahoma City in 1995 was, so he said, a response to the assaults on the Branch Davidian compound in Waco, Texas, by federal agencies two years earlier. Even what amounts to normal police conduct can, on occasion and quite unintentionally, intensify terrorist violence. The arrest and extradition to Turkey of Kurdish chieftain Abdallah Ocalan sparked a new wave of terrorism against Turkish targets throughout Europe. The killing by Israeli security services of Palestinian bomb-maker Radwan Abu Ayyash, known as "The Engineer," set off a new wave of suicide attacks that helped derail already fragile efforts at Middle East peacemaking. These examples are given recognizing that *normal police conduct* requires a certain poetic license when speaking of the Arab–Israeli conflict.

But goodwill and a desire to compromise on the part of the authorities may not work either. Since the leaders of terrorist organizations are typically radicals who regard compromise as a form of betrayal, they may react accordingly and intensify terrorism as

parties to a conflict near a settlement. In the mid-1970s, the willingness of Italy's ruling Christian Democrats to reach a historic compromise with the Communist Party led the country's Red Brigades to
escalate their violence and to strike at the heart of the state. The 1998
Good Friday agreement over Northern Ireland prompted the real
Irish Republican Army (IRA) to detonate a bomb in Armagh that left
dozens dead. In the context of the Middle East peace process, experience suggests that the closer Palestinian and Israeli negotiators come
to an agreement, the more terrorism intensifies. In Colombia in 1985
members of the revolutionary M-19 organization greeted presidential
offers of amnesty and an opportunity to participate in the peaceful
political process by invading the palace of justice in Bogota. Eleven
members of the country's Supreme Court were killed in the ensu-
ing shootout. And the urban guerrillas who took advantage of the
opportunity to come in from the cold and then to run for parliament
as reform-minded candidates were often gunned down by members
of right-wing death squads during their campaign appearances.

If all these observations about internal sources of terrorism bear
a reasonably close resemblance to the realities involved, what policy
recommendations emerge? Let us assume that whether or not a terrorist campaign begins and, if it does, how long it lasts are more
likely to be a result of instigating rather than permissive conditions. If
this inference is correct, then very close attention should be given to
the radicalization of the political arena and responses to this development by enterprising individuals—by small groups for whom terrorism represents an option and by the forces of order in the country.

Citizens of Iceland, Luxembourg, Norway, New Zealand, and a
handful of other democracies may live out their lives without fear-
ing their countries will be convulsed by political turmoil. Politics in
those countries does not take place in the streets. But most democracies, especially those Zimmermann labels noisy democracies, experience periods of mass protest and spirals of radicalization, or episodes
where outsiders directly challenge those in positions of power. The
outsiders, who use unconventional means or direct action to pose
their challenge, seem to play a perfectly normal part in the democratic experience.

Terrorism is a different matter. Authorities in democracies can do
little to prevent a small band of radicalized individuals from carrying
out a handful of terrorist attacks as an experiment to see what reactions their exemplary deeds elicit from their potential constituents
and from the forces of order. At such times the conduct of the authorities becomes crucial. Calibrating the right response no doubt requires
considerable skill. It is clear that the right response must (1) be aimed

at separating the small band from its potential mass constituency; (2) deny it the means of recruiting new generations of members; and (3) prevent it from spreading to other locations in the country.

International Terrorism and Democracies

We do not need to be reminded that democracies are also vulnerable to international terrorism. The United States and its allies seem especially attractive targets. Martha Crenshaw suggests we consider the structure of the present international system as an explanation for international terrorism against the United States and its allies, specifically that the United States is the hegemon—the unchallenged hyperpower—of the post-cold war era.[10] A self-congratulatory "We're number one" status often evokes feelings of contempt, thinly disguised envy, and unlimited hatred across the world. All three are surely among the most important motivations for terrorism. The trouble with using the present structure of the international system to explain why international terrorists target the United States is that terrorist violence against the United States and its allies also occurred when other structures prevailed. The United States and its institutions, representatives, and citizens were frequent targets of terrorist attacks when the international system was bipolar, especially during the latter decades of the cold war when Latin American urban guerrillas, European social revolutionaries, and various PLO-related organizations all found the United States to be an attractive target.

The multipolarity of the international system during the last decades of the nineteenth century and in the years leading up to World War I, as well as during the interwar period, may have meant that America was less frequently targeted by international terrorists during the period, but it hardly meant that international terrorism was absent. Virtually all the major powers of the era were subject to terrorist attacks either by international anarchists or by nationalist groups hoping to achieve the liberation of their nations from the imperial domination of one empire or another.

Globalization is another characteristic of our current condition that some believe arouses international terrorist violence. The logic here is that regions of the world where globalizing trends are felt most acutely in economic, social, and cultural terms are most likely to experience a political backlash. International terrorism, then, is one expression of such a backlash, as people most troubled by globalization lash out against the country or countries perceived as instigating it. More generally, international terrorists attack the United States and Western European countries because they oppose the economic and cultural penetration of their homelands by the West. A correlative contention about the terrorism-inducing impact of globalization concerns the immigration of large numbers of Middle Eastern and North African Muslims to the countries of Western Europe. Living among non-Muslims in such cities as Amsterdam, Hamburg, and London causes a number of stresses and strains, making young men in particular vulnerable to the appeals of Al-Qaeda and its various cells and networks.

After the bombings in Madrid March 11, 2004, and in London July 7–21, 2005, it is difficult to deny that the presence of an alientated immigrant population provided a pool from which terorists were recruited. Immigrant populations have frequently provided large pools from which so-called terrorist mosquitoes have appeared for many years. At the end of the nineteenth and beginning of the twentieth centuries, groups of Italian and, to some extent, Russian immigrants living in Argentina, France, Spain, and the United States contributed a meaningful number of violent anarchists to the historical moment, who waged terrorist campaigns against capitalism and the bourgeois state. The phenomenon thus predates the current era of globalization by close to a century.

If promoting and benefiting from globalization were a significant cause of international terrorism, then Japan, South Korea, Taiwan, and the People's Republic of China should be among the most frequent targets. But, of course, this is hardly the case. In fact, evidence points in another direction. Eubank and I compared the rankings of sixty-two countries on a recently developed index of globalization and then evaluated those rankings with the rankings of the same countries on measures of international terrorism drawn from the ITERATE III and the Rand-St. Andrews Chronologies.[11] It was discovered, in general, that a high proportion of international terrorist events occur in the world's least globalized countries. The most common type of international terrorist attack was one involving perpetrators from a country ranking low on the index of globalization who employed violence against victims or targets from another country also ranking low on this index. To the extent that citizens of countries ranking high on the measure of globalization have been victimized by international terrorism, the perpetrators of the attacks tended to come largely from other countries also ranking high on this measure. The level of lethality was not taken into consideration. But if the analysis from this study were confined to the simple frequency of international terrorist events, then it seems clear that an explanation for the current wave of international terrorism based on a reaction against globalization and countries identified as globalization's sponsors and beneficiaries is not supported by the available evidence.

To the degree that an explanation can be found or a lesson learned from the attacks in the United States on September 11, 2001, in Madrid on March 11, 2004, and in London in July 2005, it will unlikely be found in general statements about the structure of the international system or globalization. Such statements and criteria are too broad to do much good. Rather, in the search for meaning, the best explanations likely will be found in the specific expressions of those doing the killing and some features about the countries whose citizens have been targeted for murder.

If such a search is conducted while listening to what the terrorist chieftains have to say, it is not hard to identify particular foreign policies that have made the United States, along with some other democracies, targets for attack by international terrorist organizations. In the case of the United States and Al-Qaeda—and groups linked to it—the policies involved seem clear cut. Osama bin Laden and his followers were infuriated in August 1990 when the Saudi Arabia government agreed to allow the first George Bush administration to station American troops there to protect against a possible invasion by the Iraqis following Saddam Hussein's invasion of Kuwait.[12] The presence of non-Muslims inside the House of Islam—including Somalia in 1993—in addition to American support for the non-Islamic regimes in Cairo and Riyadh were the principal reasons bin Laden, Ayman al-Zawahiri (usually identified as Al-Qaeda's second in command), and their followers offered for launching terrorist attacks inter alia on the American embassies in Nairobi and Dar es Salaam, the USS Cole, and the World Trade Center. The U.S. decision to invade Iraq in March 2003 provided an additional rationale for more terrorism against American targets.[13] Concomitantly, the murderous terrorist attacks on commuter trains in Madrid and the London Underground have been linked by both the terrorist groups and their academic observers to the support the Spanish and British governments provided for the American initiative in Iraq.

Other democracies have been targets of international terrorism for reasons unrelated to their relationship to the United States. France was the site of multiple terrorist attacks during the 1990s by the Armed Islamic Group because of the French government's support for the Algerian regime, which is in the process of repressing various insurgent Islamist organizations on its own territory. Likewise, in recent years India has been struck repeatedly by such jihad groups as Lashkar e-Tayba and Harakat ul Mujahadin over its continued control of Jammu/Kashmir, a state with a Muslim majority.[14] The intractable conflict between Israel and the Palestinians also must be considered. Al-Qaeda and its various offspring have repeatedly cited

Washington's support for Israel—defined as an outpost of unbelief inside the House of Islam—as a reason for staging terrorist attacks against American targets throughout the world. It is worth noting that the principal Palestinian groups—Hamas, Palestinian Islamic Jihad, and the Al Aqsa Martyrs Brigade—presently engaged in jihad against Israel have chosen not to attack American targets. Their terrorism has been directed locally, not globally. The older and largely secular groups under the PLO umbrella (e.g., the Popular Democratic Front for the Liberation of Palestine, the Popular Front for the Liberation of Palestine-General Command, Fatah) carried out attacks against American targets in Europe and the Middle East during the late 1960s and 1970s. The context for these attacks was not global jihad but the Cold War struggle between the Soviet Union and the United States for power and influence in the Middle East; Palestinian groups received support from and often acted on behalf of the Soviet Union. In fact, Al-Qaeda is a latecomer to the struggle against Israel. Its pronouncements on the linkage between the sufferings of the Palestinians and American support for Israel followed the outbreak of the Al Aqsa Intifada in fall 2000 and the subsequent display by al-Jazeera and other Arab mass media of the Israeli military's attacks on various Palestinian targets in the West Bank and Gaza Strip.

Particular foreign policies in general and the United States in particular have made democracies the targets of international terrorism. But there is more to the story. Democracies possess certain attributes that make them vulnerable to attack. First and foremost is their defining characteristic: rule by the people. Or, to quote Osama bin Laden's November 2002 "Letter to America," "By electing these leaders, the American people have given their consent to the incarceration of the Palestinian people, the demolition of Palestinian homes, and the slaughter of the children of Iraq. The American people have the ability and choice to refuse the policies of their government, yet time and again, polls show the American people support the policies of the elected government...This is why the American people are not innocent."[15] Since the United States is a democracy, American citizens may be held collectively responsible for the actions of their government. The same logic then applies to the Spanish, British, Australian, and other democracies as well. Where the people rule, the people should be held not merely morally but also physically accountable for the actions of their governments.

Democracies also possess well-known qualities that enhance their vulnerability to international terrorist attack. Unlike, for example, the People's Republic of China or North Korea, their borders are usually permeable, making entry and exit relatively easy.

Those seeking sanctuary are usually treated humanely even when they express hatred and loathing for the very countries in which they have come to reside. Aliens usually enjoy the protection of the law. It was reported, for example, that a small military intelligence unit identified Mohammad Atta and three other 9/11 terrorists in summer 2000 and suspected them of planning attacks. The U.S. Federal Bureau of Investigation was informed of these suspicions, but it refused to pursue an investigation on the grounds these individuals held valid visas, making their stay in the country perfectly legal.[16] Democratic office-holders are sensitive to public concerns about the loss of human life. The right to privacy, the freedoms of worship and personal association, the freedom to move from one place to another within a country—in short, many values citizens prize about life in democratic countries—make them vulnerable to international terrorists who are able to exploit these values for their own ends. I am not saying that open societies and open borders make for international terrorism. Rather I assert that international terrorist bands such as Al-Qaeda's various offspring have found it relatively easy to conduct operations in democracies whose foreign policies are in conflict with their fundamental aims.

*****

In concluding this short chapter, sweeping generalizations about root causes of terrorism are of limited value. If anything, democracy seems to be a root cause in the sense that open societies and transparent governments provide conditions in which those prepared to wage terrorist campaigns may operate at least for a while. The response of the authorities within democracies requires the closest attention. At the domestic level, how they respond to a radicalized political environment and a handful of terrorist events may determine if they will then confront a large-scale and protracted terrorist campaign or simply a minor annoyance. The situation that policymakers in democracies face in dealing with international terrorist attacks poses a serious dilemma. If these attacks are triggered not by the structure of the international system in general but by specific foreign policies—for example Spanish or Australian military involvement in Iraq or French support for the Algerian government—then the solution seems easy enough. Do what the terrorists want, and their attacks will stop.

Two problems arise with this acquiescent response. First, the attacks may not stop. The departure of American forces from Somalia following the Black Hawk down incident in 1992, for example, emboldened Al-Qaeda to carry out more lethal attacks on U.S. targets: Witness the bombings of the American embassies in Nairobi and Dar es Salaam. Second, if blackmail works in one instance—if a small band of terrorists is able to compel a major power to change its foreign policy by setting off a few bombs—then other small bands with other foreign policy goals may very well do likewise. The result will not be an end to terrorism but instead an escalatory spiral involving growing violence. Acquiescing to the demands of international terrorists may perhaps yield short-term benefits, but its long-term consequences may prove another matter.

Endnotes

1. Martha Crenshaw, "The Causes of Terrorism," *Comparative Politics* 13:4 (1981): 379–91.
2. Tore Bjorgo (ed.), *The Root Causes of Terrorism* (New York: Routledge, 2004), 234–5.
3. Leonard Weinberg and William Eubank, "Does Democracy Stimulate Terrorism?" *Terrorism and Political Violence* 6, no. 4 (1994): 417–35.
4. Jan Oskar Engene, *Terrorism in Western Europe* (Northampton, MA: Edward Elgar, 2004).
5. Ibid., 79–98.
6. Ibid., 99–164.
7. Ekkart Zimmermann, "Political Unrest in Western Europe," *West European Politics* 12, no. 3 (1989): 179–96.
8. Weinberg and Eubank, "Terrorism and Changes in Political Party Systems," in *Political Parties and Terrorist Groups*, ed. Weinberg (London: Frank Cass, 1992), 125–39.
9. Ze'ev Schiff and Ehud Ya'ari, *Intifada* (New York: Simon and Schuster, 1990), 51–78.
10. Martha Crenshaw, blog circulated to members of the work group on the political causes of terrorism for the Madrid Summit on Democracy, Terrorism, and Security, March 8–11, 2004.
11. Weinberg and Eubank, "Terrorism, Globalism, and Democracy," in *Research on Terrorism: Trends, Achievements and Failures*, ed. Andrew Silke (London: Frank Cass, 2004), 91–103.
12. Daniel Benjamin and Steven Simon, *The Age of Sacred Terror* (New York: Random House, 2003), 108–9.
13. Jean Charles Brissard, *Zarqawi* (New York: The Other Press, 2005), 126–27.
14. Jessica Stern, *Terror in the Name of God* (New York: Harper Collins, 2003), 32–84.
15. Quoted in Mohammad-Mahmoud Ould Mohamedu, *Non-linearity of Engagement* (Cambridge, MA: Harvard University, 2005), 4.
16. See *New York Times*, August 9, 2005, A1.

5

Counterterrorism and Repression

Michael S. Stohl

Through acts of violence, whether perpetrated or threatened, terrorists seek to create fear or compliant behavior in a victim or an audience for the act or threat. Counterterrorism actions therefore must always address not simply the treatment of and response to actions that have taken place and the prevention of future acts of terrorism but also the reactions of the audience to the acts or threats. Authorities must thus not only make the public more secure; they must also make the public subjectively believe that they are more secure and must create confidence that the authorities are acting toward that end. Such communicative actions are necessary not only at the epicenters of terrorist activity but also in seemingly peripheral locations where the public experiences a shared empathic identity and collective loss with those stricken and also a sense of vulnerability in potentially being future victims.

The failure on the part of the authorities to make the public more secure—or at least to create a sense of security—amounts to a victory for the terrorist. But as a process, failing to create a sense of security for the public and not demonstrating that the political authorities are doing what they should often present more of a threat to the political system than particular security lapses. The fact that many terrorist threats originate outside the geographic boundaries of a particular state and that the scope of possible operations and targets may be found anywhere on the globe means that public and governmental perceptions and actions within the international community are also important. Thus, countering terrorism involves the use of all the security forces of the state within the context of a political process. It is not simply about destroying the threat; consideration should also be given to the means with which to get rid of the threat, as well as how it and the counterterror involved are perceived.

To understand the requirements of an effective counterterrorism policy we must understand that terrorism is different from other forms of violence or its threat. As difficult as it is for us to accept in the immediate aftermath of an attack with victims in plain view, terrorists are primarily interested in the audience, not the victims. Terrorism is designed to have direct and indirect victims, and it is crucial to understand that how the audience reacts is as important as the act itself and the instrumental victims who are its direct casualties. Therefore, counterterrorism policy must address not only the violence of the terrorist actor but also the multiple audiences of the violence, which may be local, national, regional, or global.

Identifying the Purposes of Counterterrorism

Counterterrorism is not as simple as winning military battles, destroying a network structure, preventing particular acts, or capturing particular terrorist actors. There is a constant interplay of fear, anger, and uncertainty that terrorists try to produce in their potential target victim audience while they also attempt to create support for their actions from those for whom they purport to speak. Counterterrorism requires authorities to attempt to provide security and reassurance that they can protect the population, can eliminate the future threat, and can discourage potential supporters of the terrorists. This process also focuses on the social identity of the audience, presenting the challenge to decide if they align with the terrorists and their government or against them; with a potential target, victim, or a bystander; with a supporter or opponent. Terrorists seek through their actions to generate responses that in addition to creating fear will induce potential recruits, will provide safe havens, will provoke a response to financial requests, and will cause support from authorities to be withdrawn. Through their counterterrorism policies authorities intend that both government supporters (and potential supporters) will provide information, back their policies and actions, and will trust that their future will be more secure by doing so. At the same time authorities intend that opponents (and potential opponents) of the government will fear that continued withholding of support for the government through their silence or continued support of the terrorists will bring them harm.

What complicates the efforts of counterterrorist agents in the contemporary global media environment is that both a state's and terrorists' actions are in public view. Terrorists do not need to attack in a particular location—although some locations are clearly better than others—to broadcast their message to audiences both near to and far from the terrorist event. Likewise, the actions of governments against terrorists, their supporters, and potentially innocent bystanders are also liable to be broadcast both at home and abroad. Counterterrorist strategy must be sensitive to, and must accommodate, the reactions of multiple publics; it also needs to exhibit a better understanding of how different segments of the community will respond to different types and locations of events, to different victims, and to potential targets. Counterterrorist strategy must therefore also be established on an understanding of how social identity affects the processing of messages of fear and security and whether such messages produce fear or anger and a greater or lesser sense of risk and uncertainty. Such understanding will aid the development of credible messages of trust and reassurance, which ideally will find expression in resilient and productive community initiatives central to success.

Terrorists also understand this, which is demonstrated in a letter published in July 2005 by Ayman al-Zawahiri, purportedly Al-Qaeda's second in command, to Abu Musab al-Zarqawi, leader of the organization now named Al-Qaeda in Iraq.

> In the absence of this popular support, the Islamic mujahed movement would be crushed in the shadows, far from the masses who are distracted or fearful, and the struggle between the Jihadist elite and the arrogant authorities would be confined to prison dungeons far from the public and the light of day. This is precisely what the secular, apostate forces that are controlling our countries are striving for. These forces don't desire to wipe out the mujahed Islamic movement, rather they are stealthily striving to separate it from the misguided or frightened Muslim masses.... Therefore, the mujahed movement must avoid any action that the masses do not understand or approve, if there is no contravention of Sharia in such avoidance, and as long as there are other options to resort to, meaning we must not throw the masses—scant in knowledge—into the sea before we teach them to swim.[1]

The implementation of counterterrorist policy is also directly influenced by the existing relationship between the public and the police and other counterterrorist agencies, as well as the public's appraisal of other governments and ethnic and religious groups. Building and maintaining trust in the agents and agencies of counterterror is a key component in the process. This involves how different communication processes are likely to affect the ability of law enforcement to success-fully carry out its counterterrorism role—that is, to affect the public's actual security—and how such communication processes may affect the public's sense of security, which terrorists seek to undermine.

When shaping counterterrorism policy, states must also remember that the reactions of the audiences are as important as their short-term elimination of particular terrorists or their capacities to act. Terrorists recognize the potential for states to overreact by ignoring their own legal requirements and norms of behavior; indeed, Carlos Marighela argued that by their actions opposition groups should try to provoke repressive and reactionary responses to demonstrate the true nature of the "oppressive regime."[2]

Counterterrorism at Home

At the Madrid Summit, a number of suggestions were made for coun-tering and combating insurgent terrorism. Underlying the recommen-dations was the conviction that democracy and democratic processes were at the heart of both the terrorist threat and core components of a successful response. The general view also emerged that whatever action needed to be taken should fully apply democratic principles and absolute respect for the rule of law. These evaluations were based not just on a normative preference for democracy but also on the conviction that the underlying principles of democracy and the rule of law provide the best foundation for policy choices. An expected utility approach provides important insights into how democratic processes will contribute to successful counterterrorism policies and how ignoring democratic norms and process will—particularly in the longer term—harm counterterrorism efforts by democratic states. The expected utility approach locates counterterrorism as a set of strategic actions in a conflict situation. Within this frame, authorities and terrorists calculate the benefits they would accrue by choosing particular policies and weigh them against the probability of success and the costs of undertaking the policy so as to determine if the ben-efits exceed the risks. The policy choices may be directed at eliminat-ing, quieting, or mitigating an actual or perceived potential challenge or threat on the part of some identifiable terrorists, either domestic or international. Repression and other forms of human rights violations may be part of the set of choices—the tool box from which authori-ties may choose. As Christian Davenport argued, when repression and human rights violations are calculated as relatively more effec-tive means of governance, then the government might choose repres-sive behaviors "when the value for quiescence and the probability of success are high and the costs are low. Governments are less likely to violate human rights, however, when the value of quiescence and the probability of success are low and the costs are high."[3] The same logic applies when states conduct operations beyond their borders.

Ted Gurr outlined three sets of conditions, which affect the decision-making calculus of threatened elites: situational, structural, and dispositional.[4] Situational conditions include the political traits of challenges—the status and strategies of challengers—and the elites' own political resources for countering those challenges—regime strength and police apparatus. Structural conditions define elites' relations with their opponents and determine or constrain their response options. These include states' position in the international system and the nature of social stratification and elites' position within it. Dispositional conditions can be expected to influence how elites regard the acceptability of strategies of violence and terrorism. Norms supporting the use of violence are shaped by elites' direct or mediated experience with violent means of power and are inhibited by democratic values.

A significant aspect of the debate within democracies as to the approach to take to responding to terrorism concerns the capacity of the state to withstand the threat. The debate is long-standing. Paul Wilkinson argued that the threat to order presented by terrorists necessitates strong measures that will protect the rule of law and societal order. J. Bowyer Bell responded that a democratic society's refuge was in the rule of law and warned to beware of "apostles of order" as special pleaders with other motives in mind. Simplifying greatly, Bell and Wilkinson may represent the two competing tensions within the liberal approach to politics: law and order. Bell seeks order through established law; Wilkinson sees law established by an initial establishment of order.[5]

Bell suggested that an appropriate response to the further threat of terrorism consists of a scrupulous reliance on the law, taking care not to overreact nor to violate or to dispense with civil liberties. Ultimately it means not only recognizing but also accepting that no way exists to protect open societies at all times from violent individuals. Wilkinson concluded that "the government has a duty to invoke special powers to protect the community, restore order, and reestablish the rule of law." Bell countered that "if we cannot tolerate the exaggerated horror flashed on the evening news or the random bomb without recourse to the tyrant's manual—then we do not deserve to be free."[6] The Wilkinson–Bell debate is mirrored in the recent past in the work of Philip Heymann and Alan Dershowitz, among many others, and the debates within democratic societies about the need for additional powers, special powers, or the suspension of long-held constitutional principles or guarantees or both.[7]

Using State Power

Even though the choices are difficult when arguing about the part of the counterterrorism process involving managing the threat of attack and the tactical response, it is important to remember that it is just one part of the counterterrorist strategic requirements. As indicated previously, it is also important to manage the issues of identity, trust, support, and fear and to understand how the use, misuse, and perceptions of misuse, of state power affect the responses of the counterterrorism audiences.

The expected utility approach suggests that the management of terrorism should be based on increasing the costs and on reducing the benefits of the option. Jeffrey Ross and Gurr discuss four general kinds of conditions that can contribute to the decline of political terrorism: preemption, deterrence, burnout, and backlash. "Preemption and deterrence are counterterrorist policies and actions which can reduce or eliminate the terrorists' coercive capabilities. Burnout and backlash are general conditions which reduce the political capabilities of groups using terrorism."[8] Thus far the focus of much of the post-September 11, 2001, counterterrorism response has been heavily military and has focused on the production side of the equation— that is, on the preemption and deterrence options identified by Ross and Gurr. I suggest that increasing the response cost part of the equation, including burnout and backlash, is of equal and perhaps potentially greater benefit in the long run.

Burnout refers to members' declining commitment to the group and its purposes, an effect more frequently seen and pronounced in ideological movements. As in all militant organizations, it is reinforced over time by the aging of members of the terrorist organization. The greatest numbers are recruited in their teens and twenties and begin departing in their thirties as they lose hope in "making a difference" and seek to "live their life".[9] In ideological networks, organizational members are far less likely to be embedded in a homophilous multiplex set of familial, or kinship, relations that socializes, reinforces, and supports or even is aware of the terrorist organization. Therefore, it is far more likely that discrepant messages, alternative interpretations, and diverse options will become visible and viable for the organizational member. Thus, policies that can contribute to burnout by providing economic incentives and alternatives should be of great utility, although they will not be as useful against organizations based on family, clan, or other strong ties.[10]

A successful counterterrorism policy creates backlash against actors who choose to employ terrorism. Backlash refers to actions that antagonize and alienate the terrorist organizations from the larger sociopolitical context in which they are embedded and are interdependent. These strategies seek to delegitimize the actions of terrorists. Accommodative political strategies initiated by governments as a response to terrorist threats or actions may serve to reduce the acquiescence of societies to terrorists in their midst if organizational leaders do not respond positively or accept the gains offered by authorities. Accommodative offers, as minimal as they might be, may offer the hope of a continued presence in the political agenda. They force populations not directly linked to the organization but whose support or acquiescence is vital to the organizations' survival to consider whether continued adherence to the ultimate goals of the organization or continuing tolerance for the right to exist is worth the everyday effects of the continued presence of terrorists. Such a rational calculation brought on by official governmental action is more likely to create backlash from the wider society undermining the political capabilities of doctrinal terrorist movements than those of clan or ethnonationalist organizations. Within such a communicative context, it is easier for governmental actions to isolate the organization—but only if it does not engage in activities characterized by opponents as terrorist. Ethan Bueno de Mesquita sounded a cautionary note that concessions may bring initial escalation because more extreme elements are the only ones remaining but that "the benefits of counterterrorism aid from former terrorists may outweigh the costs of heightened militancy."[11]

Hence, it is not surprising that terrorist movements showing decline—and in many cases disappearance altogether—over the past thirty years have been the ideologically based movements such as the Red Army Faction; Action Directe in France; and the Red Brigades of Germany, France, and Italy. In contrast, terrorist groups that have shown the greatest resilience are the ethnonationalist movements such as the Basque Fatherland and Liberty, the Sri Lankan-based Liberation Tigers of Tamil Eelam, the Irish Republican Army, and the numerous Palestinian groups. In the former, a combination of successful intelligence and police work, the ability to isolate the terrorists from the population, inducements to encourage disengagement, and burnout all worked together to end the movements. In the latter, the continued political stalemates and the ability of the terrorists to maintain their reservoir of support within the communities they attempt to represent has meant that they have been able to continue to recruit and to find a safe haven there; over time, they also develop fuller organizational presences.

Backlash

When considering the process of backlash, it is important to recognize that we are also attempting to delegitimize the terrorist option. It is necessary to tear away at the protective clothing that allows oppositional organizations, their publics, and the states that support them to ignore the human consequences such terrorist behavior generates. If such behavior is delegitimized, the psychological production costs are increased for decision makers and for those who support them. By challenging the behavior and by raising public awareness at home and abroad we increase the possibilities of bystanders of the terrorism challenging terrorist behaviors and support for them. Examining political organizations in different geographic, cultural, and historic settings considering the wide variance in circumstance and contending political and social groupings, and employing an expected utility approach forces us to contend with the willingness of many different political organizations to use not just violence but also victims instrumentally. By thinking about the processes and structures that constrain such behaviors, it is clear that calculations about the response by enemies as well as supporters are a key component in restraining the instrumental use of victims. As Jack Goldstone suggested, "The actions and reactions of regimes, regime opponents, counter-movements, and the broader public all reshape the processes of group identification, perceptions of the efficacy and justice of the regime and its opponents, and estimates of what changes are possible."[12]

Counterterror strategies need to address the response of the communities terrorists purport to represent and to choose tactics that encourage backlash against—rather than further support for—terrorists. One such strategic response that is always tempting for governments is repression. Policies of repression employ the use of or the threat of coercion against opponents and potential opponents to prevent or weaken their capability to oppose the authorities and their policies. This coercion may use the full machinery of the state, including the judiciary as well as the police and military. The state may also deny social and economic privileges to whole classes of people, thereby also preventing the enjoyment of basic human rights outlined in the Universal Declaration. There is no question that in the short term governmental repression can produce reluctance on the part of the audience to support terrorism conducted in its name. Repression raises the costs for known supporters and creates much greater caution in acquiescing to the violent claims. However, increased repression over time may actually generate increased collective actions. Often, paradoxically, fierce repression is unable to daunt—or even inflames—revolutionary opposition.[13]

To illustrate, David Mason and Dale Krane, based on their analysis of El Salvador, argued that indiscriminate repression may increase opposition to the regime. Violent repression erodes the popular legitimacy of the regime, precludes the use of more conventional nonviolent modes of participation, and thereby compels the opposition to resort to violence intended not simply bring about changes in government policy or personnel but also to force a revolutionary change of regime.[14] Likewise, Peter Chalk in his examination of Southeast Asia argued that the repression conducted by the governments has compounded the sense of dissatisfaction and has fueled separatist movements and created greater support.[15] Likewise, Bruno Coppieter stressed that "from the perspective of legitimate authority, the indiscriminate and disproportionate use of force and repression by the Russian authorities, and the lack of criminal proceedings against those who perpetrated war crimes, undermine the legitimacy of the Russian government and the authority of those Chechens who are ready to cooperate with the Russian government."[16] Examining the behavior of Hamas, Saul Mishal compared Hamas's response to the repression under Israeli hands to the behavior of other Islamic movements, such as the Muslim Brothers groups in Jordan and Sudan, which tend to be reformist rather than revolutionary, generally preferring to operate overtly and legally "unless forced to go underground and use subversive or violent methods in response to severe repression.[17] Commonality seems to exist across cultures, time, and space so that one long-term result of repressive policies is a continuation of support for violence committed in the name of groups mobilizing against terrorism. Repression, though often apparently successful in the short run, can serve to fill the very reservoirs of support it is designed to empty.

Building Transnational Counterterrorism Networks

When we move beyond the confines of individual states these same principles still apply. States confronted by the threat of transnational insurgent terror recognize the need to collaborate with other states to eliminate safe havens, to control financial resources, and to guard and to prevent the sales of weapons and explosives. After September 11, for example, the U.S. government, using both figurative carrots (e.g., resources, aid, weapons) and sticks (e.g., threats to withhold financial aid), put pressure on numerous governments to connect terrorists acting within their borders to the global terror network.

However, one of the problems for democracies engaged in attempting to build transnational counterterrorism networks is that many of the nations whose assistance was thought necessary in the global war against terror were not democracies, and were engaged in the systematic violation of their citizens' human rights and often used repression against their citizens to maintain their regimes. Amnesty International and Human Rights Watch have documented numerous abuses in Uzbekistan, Tajikistan, Turkmenistan, Azerbaijan, Kazakhstan, Kyrgyzstan, and Georgia within the Central Asian region. These regimes routinely suppress internal dissent, arrest political opponents, and censor the media. Political dissent of any kind is harshly suppressed, and beatings and torture of detainees is commonplace.

Additionally, some nations sought entrance into the coalition for their own domestic purposes as well. China, for example, lobbied for ten months to have the East Turkistan Islamic Movement added to the U.S. list of terrorist organizations linked to Osama bin Laden's global terror network.[18] To many external observers, as well as to the populations within these new allies, the actions of the democracies' new partners appear purely opportunistic, declaring their intention to fight the global terror network merely to aid in their elimination of unconnected challenges to their own regimes.

However, the problem is not just that these governments will repress their own people. It is also important to recognize in a globally capable information society that a strategy of delegitimization is connected to counterterrorism policies and partnerships as well. Counterterrorism policies and coalitions that involve assisting or enlisting so-called bad governments—that is, governments that repress their populations or use their powers to discriminate with respect to the distribution of goods and opportunities across ethnic divides—might not always create dissonance across the entire audience in the nations engaged in the global war on terror. However, these counterterrorism policies are bound to create the wrong kind of backlash in societies mirroring the conditions that support organizations using terror in their homeland or abroad. Just as the black–white mentality of the cold war created pressures to support bad governments on "our" side and thus condemned populations within those societies to repression and underdevelopment, the War on Terror has the potential to do the same in the west, central, and inner Asian former Soviet republics and elsewhere.[19] However, in today's globalized media environment the results are shared not only on CNN and the BBC but also on Al Jazeera and on the web in front of the populations shielding, or acquiescing to, the terrorists in their midst. Any counterterrorism policy or action that lowers the response costs for terrorist organizers and their supportive populations reduces the potential effectiveness of the policy or action.

Thus when states sell, grant, and otherwise provide favorable terms by which their coalition partners, allies, client states (and at times neutrals and even adversaries) obtain equipment which enables regimes to continue and/or expand practices of repression and terrorism, or engage in training the personnel that conducts the terror operations, audiences both in their own states and in these nations are witness to these policy choices. As the Madrid discussions emphasized, democracies need to undermine the terrorist appeal to the populations of countries from whom they need to draw their support and/or acquiescence if insurgent terrorists are to have fewer places in which to find safe haven. They will find this more difficult if they appear to support policies of repression and terror by governments against the populations to whom they are appealing.

In the interconnected global environment in which transnational terrorism is confronted, a counterterrorist coalition seeking to mobilize multiple populations must have trust as an important component. In a general sense it is always important for democracies to show the utmost respect for the principles on which they stand, including truth and justice. In that context the abuses of Abu Ghraib and Guantánamo, the policy of rendition, all reduce the respect of the populations within the historically democratic nations and feed into the propaganda of Al-Qaeda about the willingness of the United States and the West to systematically deny the same rights and respect to the people Al-Qaeda purports to represent. U.S. leadership in the global war on terror is accompanied by arguments built on American Exceptionalism. This exceptionalism is exemplified, for example, by the doctrine of preemption introduced in the 2002 National Security Strategy and in the refusal to join the International Criminal Court. This assertion of exceptionalism may undercut the ability to counter the message of the terrorists and fracture the support of the populations with other democratic partners as well. As Darren Davis and Brian Silver noted, trust in government is a resource on which governments may draw.[20] Indeed, low levels of trust make it more difficult for governments to succeed. The populations of the democratic states must trust that the governments of the counterterrorism network will act in good faith. Heymann, addressing an American audience, suggested that "we must learn never to react to the limited violence of small groups by launching a crusade in which we destroy our unity as a nation or our trust in the fairness and restraint of the institutions of the U.S. government that control legitimate force."[21] This is advice a counterterrorism coalition of democratic nations must heed.

However serious the threat of terrorism they must not yield the rule of law to combat it.

In closing, it is useful to ponder the observations of Jeffrey Goldfarb, codeveloper with Adam Michnik, of the "Democracy Seminar which takes place twice a year in Krakow and Cape Town and brings together students and activists to discuss the creation and sustenance of democratic structures." He reports on the reactions of students—the very ones he says should be the best allies the United States has in the long run—to the development of the counterterrorism network. These students say:

> It is the war on terrorism that is being used as cover by dictators around the world to justify crackdown on democracy advocates. Suddenly the rights of Muslims in the Philippines and Indonesia—or the democratic critics of the authoritarian "Asian way" in Singapore, Malaysia and Burma—are not important to the Bush administration. Suddenly the strategic resources of Central Asian dictatorships are more important than the lives of human rights activitists. Suddenly the defense of the American way of life and our democracy seems to be predicated upon a lack of concern for the democratic rights of people in less advantage countries.[22]

If the policies of the counterterrorism coalition and the disregard of the United States for the audience of those policies have created such views in potential friends of the United States, the long-term success of a strategy that does not place its adherence to its most basic principles at its core is much in doubt. Repression and the denial of human rights will only harm the counterterrorism struggle. Democracy and democratic processes must be the core components of a successful counterterrorism strategy and coalition.

Endnotes

1. For the full text, see http://www.dni.gov/letter_in_english.pdf.
2. Carlos Marighela, *For the Liberation of Brazil* (Harmondsworth, UK: Penguin, 1971), 113.
3. Christian Davenport, "Human Rights and the Democratic Proposition," *Journal of Conflict Resolution* 43, no. 1 (1999): 92–116.
4. Ted Robert Gurr, "The Political Origins of State Violence and Terror: A Theoretical Analysis," in *Government Violence and Repression: An Agenda for Research*, ed. Michael Stohl and George Lopez (Westport, CT: Greenwood Press, 1986), 62–7.
5. See Paul Wilkinson, *Terrorism and the Liberal State* (London: Halstead, 1977); and John B. Bell, *A Time of Terror: How Democratic*

Societies Respond to Revolutionary Violence (New York: Basic Books, 1978).

6. Wilkinson, *Terrorism*, 156; Bell, *Time of Terror*, 279.
7. Philip B. Heymann, Terrorism and America: A Commonsense Strategy for a Democratic Society (Cambridge, MA: MIT Press, 1998); and Alan M. Dershowitz, "Is There a Tortuous Route to Justice?" *Los Angeles Times*, November 8, 2001.
8. Jeffrey Ian Ross and Gurr, "Why Terrorism Subsides: A Comparative Study of Canada and the United States," *Comparative Politics* 21, no. 4 (1989): 408.
9. Charles A. Russell and Bowman Miller, "Profile of a Terrorist," *Terrorism* 1, no. 1 (1977): 18; and Neil Livingston, *The War against Terrorism* (Lexington, MA: Heath Lexington, 1982), 43–5.
10. Stohl, "Is the Past Prologue? Terrorists and WMD," *International Studies Review* 7, no. 1 (2005): 146–8.
11. Ethan Bueno de Mesquita, "Conciliation, Counterterrorism, and Patterns of Terrorist Violence," *International Organization* 59, no. 1 (2005): 146.
12. Jack A. Goldstone, "Toward a Fourth Generation of Revolutionary Theory," *Annual Review of Political Science* 4, no. 1 (2001): 139–87.
13. See Davenport, "Human Rights."
14. David Mason and Dale Krane, "The Political Economy of Death Squads: Toward a Theory of the Impact of State-Sanctioned Terror," *International Studies Quarterly* 33, no. 2 (1989): 192.
15. See Peter Chalk, "Separatism and Southeast Asia: The Islamic Factor in Southern Thailand, Mindanao, and Aceh," Studies in Conflict & Terrorism 24, no. 1 (2001): 241–69.
16. Bruno Coppieter, "Secession and War: A Moral Analysis of the Russian–Chechen Conflict," *Central Asian Survey* 22, no. 4 (2003): 393.
17. See Shaul Mishal, "The Pragmatic Dimension of the Palestinian Hamas: A Network Perspective," *Armed Forces and Society* 29, no. 4 (2003): 569–90.
18. "American Gives Beijing Good News: Rebels on Terror List," *New York Times*, August 27, 2002.
19. Anatol Lieven, "The Secret Policemen's Ball: The United States, Russia, and the International Order after Sept. 11," *International Affairs* 78, no. 2 (2002): 250.
20. Darren W. Davis and Brian Silver, "Civil Liberties vs. Security: Public Opinion in the Context of the Terrorist Attacks on America," *American Journal of Political Science* 48 (2004): 30.
21. Heymann, Terrorism in America, 158.
22. "Losing Our Best Allies in the War on Terror," *New York Times*, August 21, 2002.

6

The Causes of Revolutionary Terrorism

Ignacio Sánchez-Cuenca

Speculation about the origins of terrorism is risky, if only because the role of contingency is bigger than in other forms of political violence, such as interstate or civil wars. Given the fact that they are clandestine organizations, terrorist groups are smaller in size than national armies or guerrillas. The creation of a terrorist organization may be decided by a handful of people, and a hundred volunteers may be more than enough to launch a terrorist campaign. Whether the decisions of such a small number of people can be explained along similar lines to other, more systematic, political events—for example, the relationship between electoral rules and the number of political parties or economic development and the survival of democratic regimes—is a contentious issue.

As a result of the contingent nature of terrorism, it is probably futile to expect that the social sciences can establish some combination of necessary and sufficient conditions that bring about terrorism. Yet I suggest that we can gain some useful insights if we accept that this form of political violence is—to borrow a biological analogy—a mixture of chance and necessity. More specifically, I argue that the formation of terrorist organizations is a random mutation that occurs within societies but that some political conditions filter or select which of these mutations survive and reproduce, thus creating a serious challenge to the political system. According to this model of political selection, the formation of terrorist groups is a contingent event, but their survival or extinction is determined by conditions that can be worked out systematically.

To illustrate how chance and necessity are related in the production of terrorism, this chapter focuses on the wave of terrorist activity that started in the late '60s and early '70s in the developed world. Many countries at that time had to face the terrorist challenge. There was nationalist terrorism like in Northern Ireland or the Basque Country, revolutionary terrorism like in Italy, Germany, Japan, and Spain, and fascist, or black, terrorism like in Italy, Spain, and Portugal. Moreover, many countries did not have any terrorism at all, or had very little, like in the Scandinavian countries, the Netherlands, Belgium, France, Canada, the United States, and Australia. There is a significant variation, therefore, which I try to explain by using the political selection model.

My approach is slightly different from that of Jan Oskar Engene, who in 2004 published a study of terrorism in Western Europe.[1] First, I deal only with revolutionary terrorism, for different types of terrorism require different conditions to survive and reproduce. Second, my analysis includes all the countries in the developed world, whereas Engene's analysis was restricted to Western Europe. And third, and most importantly, I provide more accurate figures about numbers of fatalities drawn from my own data set.[2]

Terrorism can be understood in at least two different ways: as an action-based concept or as one that focuses on the actors. In the action sense, terrorism is a form of violence—mainly against civilians, often in indiscriminate attacks, trying to instill fear in a wider audience—that can be carried out by different actors, such as terrorist organizations, guerrillas, or armies. In the actor sense, terrorism is the activity displayed by terrorist organizations. Terrorist groups are different from other insurgencies because they do not control any territory, act within the enemy's territory, and hence have to be secret or underground. Guerrillas, by contrast, liberate some territory from the state's control and act in this territory like a protostate (e.g., extracting rents, imposing order). In this chapter I refer to terrorism exclusively in the actor sense. I am interested in understanding the conditions under which these organizations emerge.

In the following, I first show that the terrorist mutation of the '70s was all pervasive: small groups in favor of armed struggle could be found in almost every country in the developed world. I then examine the factors, both contingent and structural, that could explain why terrorism was more widespread in some countries than in others. Finally, there is a brief discussion about the possibility of extending the model to other instances of terrorism.

Mutation

The political mobilization of students and workers in many countries of the developed world during the second half of the '60s gave rise—

in some of them—to a wave of terrorist political violence that lasted for thirty years or even longer. Most of this violence was inspired by extreme left-wing ideology. Violence was believed to serve as an inspiration: The masses would follow the path set by the vanguard and take up arms. Even the nationalist terrorist organizations that emerged at that time—the ETA (Euskadi ta Askatasuna, Basque Homeland and Freedom) in the Basque country or the Provisional Irish Republican Army (PIRA) in Northern Ireland—incorporated Marxist jargon into their discourse.

In fact, the first instances of revolutionary terrorism took place in Latin America. The Tupamaros in Uruguay were the first to theorize and to put into practice the kind of urban guerrilla associated with the terrorism of that period. The Tupamaros attempted to emulate other Latin American guerrillas, but the absence of both mountains and jungle in their country persuaded them that it was impossible to start their rebellion in the countryside. Consequently, they concluded that their only chance was to utilize the urban environment.[3] Their example was followed by the Montoneros and other groups in Argentina. The doctrine behind this form of terrorism was systematized by the Brazilian terrorist Carlos Marighella in his *Minimanual of the Urban Guerrilla*.[4] These Latin American experiences were a source of inspiration for many revolutionary movements in Europe. A case in point is the Red Army Faction, also known as the Baader-Meinhoff group, which explicitly tried to reproduce in West Germany the urban guerilla example set forth by the Tupamaros.

In Europe, the first organizations that turned to violence were nationalist ones: The ETA killed its first victim in 1968; the schism within the IRA took place at the end of 1969; and the PIRA began to carry out assassinations in 1970.[5] The two organizations, ETA and PIRA, have lasted longer than any other and have killed far more than their contemporaries. The ETA has cost the lives of 773 people, and the PIRA 1,778.[6] Still, nationalist organizations are somewhat peculiar for a general cross-country comparison, as they only emerge in countries where regions have territorial claims. Instead of restricting the analysis to countries with this territorial cleavage, I focus mainly on left-wing, revolutionary terrorism, for this kind of terrorism—unlike the nationalist one—depends on a political cleavage present in every country of the developed world.

As mentioned before, two stages of terrorism seem to be of relevance: mutation and selection. Regarding mutation, it is possible to show that even in the countries that did not suffer from serious revolutionary terrorism from 1970-1990, there were some terrorist groups that had the same political preferences and organizational resources of those found in Italy, Spain, or Greece, yet they refused to kill people or—even if they did— were quickly disbanded by the police because of their lack of social support.

Let us examine four countries that did not suffer lethal revolutionary terrorism: Great Britain, the United States, Belgium, and the Netherlands. In each of these cases, it is possible to find a terrorist mutation that soon became extinct. In Great Britain, an underground group called the Angry Brigade was active during the early '70s. It fully rejected capitalism and imperialism and believed in revolution and armed struggle, but its members attacked property rather than people. They were easily neutralized by the police. In one of their communiqués, commenting on nonlethal attacks against four different persons, they felt it was necessary to explain that their targets "would all be dead if we had wished."[7] The question is why they did not wish to kill them.

The United States has several of these mutations in its history. The best known is the Weather Underground, a clandestine group of young people that had strong revolutionary preferences but decided not to kill anyone after the death of three of their own activists who were manipulating an explosive device in New York City in 1970. Another group, the Symbionese Liberation Army, killed two people, but its members were quickly captured by the police; the United Freedom Front killed one person.[8] None of these organizations became a source of serious concern for the United States.

In Belgium, the Communist Combatant Cells, a small, violent, revolutionary group that acted in the '80s, did not want to assassinate anyone either, though in 1985 they killed two firefighters accidentally. In the Netherlands several ultra leftist groups, like the Red Youth or its successor the Red Resistance Front, held radical views and were influenced by Carlos Marighella's writings on the urban guerrilla but did not evolve into lethal terrorism.

These examples reveal that some individuals and groups in these countries possessed strong antisystem preferences and were willing to employ violent tactics but fell short of full terrorism or were quickly disbanded after the first killings. Similar groups in other countries had a very different trajectory: bloodier and longer. The difference between the revolutionaries in the Netherlands and Italy does not lie in ideological preferences or in the organizational features of these groups but rather deals with the political system. For reasons still needing to be disentangled, the conditions of Italian politics favored the development and reproduction of these leftist, underground organizations, whereas Dutch politics constituted a hostile environment.

Political Selection

It is important to distinguish terrorist revolutionary organizations according to their degree of lethality. It would be odd to count France and Italy as having gone through the same experience: Action Directe in France assassinated twelve people, whereas the Red Brigades in Italy killed fifty-three. Table 6.1 divides countries into three categories: those that had very little revolutionary terrorism or none at all (no group killed more than five people); those with groups that killed between five and twenty people; and those where terrorist groups killed more than twenty people. Note that the criterion is not the aggregate number of fatalities in the country overall but the presence of at least one terrorist group that killed with a certain intensity. For instance, in the case of France, I take into account only Action Directe's killings in the '80s without considering the killings in the '70s by minor organizations like the Brigates Internationales (International Brigades) (two killings) or the Noyaux Armés pour l'Autonomie Populaire (Armed Nuclei for Popular Autonomy) (one killing).

Table 6.1

The impact of revolutionary terrorism in the developed world

Degree of revolutionary terrorism		
None (Less than 5 Fatalities)	Some (Between 5 and 20 Fatalities)	Intense (More than 20 Fatalities)
Australia	France	Germany
Austria	Japan	Greece
Belgium	Portugal	Italy
Canada		Spain
Denmark		
Finland		
Great Britain		
Ireland		
Netherlands		
New Zealand		
Norway		
Sweden		
Switzerland		
United States		

Excluding small countries (Iceland, Luxembourg) and Latin America, Table 6.1 contains twenty-one countries of the Western, developed world. Revolutionary terrorism was an important phenomenon in seven countries—that is, one-third of the sample. It was particularly worrisome in Italy, Spain, and Germany, in terms both of fatalities and the political strain it produced. Greece also appears in the group of countries afflicted by intense terrorism: The Revolutionary Organization 17 November killed twenty-two people during a long span of twenty-five years, though arguably it did not have as much political impact as the Red Brigades in Italy, Grupo de Resistencia Antifascista Primero de Octubre (First of October Antifascist Resistance Group) (GRAPO) in Spain, or the Red Army Faction (RAF) in Germany.

Table 6.2 contains a more detailed impression of the terrorist organizations that acted in these seven countries. The GRAPO, a Maoist group very active during the transition to democracy in Spain, is the deadliest organization, followed by the Red Brigades. Terrorism in Italy was extremely fragmented—just like the party system—and the Red Brigades and Prima Linea [Front Line] were the two main groups, with fifty-three and sixteen fatalities, respectively, out of a total of 149 fatalities caused by the extreme left.

To account for the fact that the terrorist mutation found a niche in seven of the twenty-one countries, it is convenient to separate contingent and structural factors. Contingent factors are such things as the size of the popular mobilization of the late '60s and early '70s, the presence of extreme right-wing terrorism, or the response of the state. Structural factors refer to more permanent features of the country, like economic development or the political nature of the state. Of course, the combination of contingent and structural factors requires statistical analysis. In this contribution, though, I limit myself to discussing this issue in a conventional comparative way, drawing on some of the findings of my own statistical research.

Contingent factors

Regarding the cycle of political mobilization, it is apparent from Table 6.1 that almost all of the countries where demonstrations were massive and occasionally violent ended up with revolutionary terrorism (e.g., France, Italy, Japan, Germany). The important exception is the United States, where the student movement was extremely powerful, galvanized by the Vietnam War, but where terrorism did not become an issue at all. The case of France, on the other hand, is intriguing. The 1968 mobilization was enormous, to the point that when workers joined students the country was paralyzed; however, terrorism

Table 6.2

Main revolutionary terrorist organizations

Name	Country	Total Number of Fatalities	Year of First Fatality	Year of Last Fatality
GRAPO	Spain	79	1975	2000
Brigate Rosse	Italy	53	1974	1981
RAF	Germany	34	1971	1993
17 November	Greece	22	1975	2000
Prima Linea	Italy	16	1976	1981
FP 25 Abril	Portugal	15	1980	1986
Action Directe	France	12	1980	1986

Note: The Japanese Red Army was not included given the difficulties of providing accurate figures about its activity. First, most of their killings took place outside of Japan. Second, on Japanese soil they killed more of their own members than other people. It is not clear whether internal killings should be included.

was absent in the '70s. It only emerged in the '80s, with Action Directe, and it was a rather marginal event. If political mobilization during the '60s was a relevant factor, France and the United States are two countries expected to have more terrorism, yet little to none can be found.

It cannot be by chance that Italy and Spain—the two countries where revolutionary terrorism was more lethal—are the countries where fascist terrorism was important.[9] I do not mean the kind of xenophobic, neo-Nazi violence that spread during the '80s and '90s but instead the strategy of tension oriented toward the breakdown of the democratic system. This type of violence was intended to create a situation of chaos that would offer a pretext for the army to launch a coup. In Italy two coup attempts, organized by a coalition of fascist groups and elements of the army, failed in 1970 and 1973. The tension that was to justify the coup was created through indiscriminate attacks against civilians. The bloodiest of these attacks were the Piazza Fontana bomb in Milan in December 1969, producing seventeen fatalities, the bomb explosion on the Italicus train in 1974, causing twelve fatalities, and the Bologna train station bomb in 1980, responsible for eighty-three fatalities. During these years, there were also many selective attacks against activists of ultra leftist groups. In Spain, on the other hand, the fascist attacks were mainly selective. Particularly shocking was the killing of four labor lawyers of the Communist union, the Comisiones Obreras, in January 1977, just a few months before the first democratic elections after the end of Francisco Franco's dictatorship.

The existence of fascist violence triggered the emergence of leftist organizations. It created a visible aggressor and lent credibility to the thesis held by the extreme left that Western democracies were only a facade of authoritarian regimes. The Italian terrorists of the '70s saw themselves as the heirs of the Resistance. One of the first groups that emerged in the early '70s was Grupo d'Azione Partigiana (Group of Partisan Action), created by the famous publisher Giangiacomo Feltrinelli, who—following the Piazza Fontana attack—thought that only armed struggle could prevent the return of fascism. In Spain, the GRAPO frequently justified its attacks by referring to the ongoing fascist nature of the Spanish state. For them, the connections between the security forces and fascist groups proved that despite elections Spain was still a dictatorial, oligarchic regime. Still, although fascist terrorism may have intensified leftist terrorism, it can hardly be the whole story, for we can observe revolutionary violence in other countries like Germany or Greece where fascist terrorism was absent. This suggests that, apart from political mobilization and fascism, the state's response to the cycle of popular mobilization was important as well.

The pattern of repression at the beginning of the conflict may help to account for variations in the degree of lethality.[10] Indiscriminate or excessive repression (e.g., random detentions, states of emergency, torture, excessive use of force in demonstrations and street fights) may backfire, inducing people to join terrorist organizations; this was clearly the case for nationalist terrorism. The strength of the ETA was derived to a large extent from the police repression of Basque nationalists under Franco, especially after the first killing in 1968. Likewise, in Northern Ireland, the PIRA emerged in the middle of harsh police repression and harassment by Protestants against Catholics who participated in the civil rights movement. In Italy, the police killed many students in demonstrations. The death of the anarchist Pino Pinnelli in prison in 1970, who was falsely accused of the Piazza Fontana bomb, was crucial in the perception among radicals that the state was going to use any means to put an end to the revolutionary movements. Also, during the Spanish transition many people died in fights with security forces.

The police displayed a very different behavior both in France and in Great Britain, where very little to no revolutionary terrorism is observed. Thus, in France no one was killed during spring 1968; consequently, in the following years not even the most radical groups thought killing was justified. And if we leave aside the Troubles in Northern Ireland, the fact is that both the demonstrations and the police response were quite peaceful in Great Britain.

There seems to be, therefore, some association between repression and the emergence of terrorism. However, it is difficult to test this idea rigorously without some quantitative measurement of repression. And there are some noteworthy exceptions. For example, in the United States repression was higher and more indiscriminate than in, say, Germany, but terrorism did not spread. Events like the killing of four unarmed students at Ohio's Kent State University by the National Guard, or the killing of another two students at Jackson State University in Mississippi by the police, both in 1970, did not induce terrorist organizations to launch violent campaigns.

This brief overview of contingent factors—political mobilization, fascist terrorism, state repression—shows that none of them can be taken as either necessary or sufficient. Exceptions can be found in each case: Political mobilization was low in Spain or Greece during the late '60s; there was no fascist terrorism in Germany; and repression was high in the United States. Yet Spain, Greece, and Germany had important revolutionary terrorism, but the United States did not have any. These factors should therefore be regarded as independent variables, increasing the probability that the terrorist mutation will survive and expand in certain countries, rather than as necessary or sufficient conditions.

Structural factors

Two structural factors can explain why terrorism finds a niche in some countries: the level of economic development and the nature of the state. With regard to economic development, a quick glance at Table 6.1 reveals that there is no obvious relationship between terrorism and per capita income. Among the countries that suffered revolutionary terrorism, some were clearly poorer than the average (e.g., Greece, Portugal, Spain), whereas others were quite wealthy (e.g., France, Germany, Japan). It is true, however, that poorer countries—with the exception of the Republic of Ireland—had revolutionary terrorism. Statistically, the correlation is 0.4, significant at 10 percent. Importantly, though, the correlation disappears once we control for the nature of the state. The classification of countries in Table 6.1 suggests a strong association between the emergence of revolutionary terrorism and countries with a dictatorial past. Of the seven countries with revolutionary terrorism, six went through right-wing authoritarian regimes during the twentieth century. France is the only exception, unless we consider, as some people do, that the Vichy years were an authoritarian parenthesis.[11] And among the countries that did not have revolutionary terrorism, all were democracies without any breakdown except Austria.

Why would countries with a dictatorial past provide a niche for the terrorist mutation? In some of the cases, the authoritarian past was very recent—in Greece and Portugal until 1974 and in Spain until 1975—and it is only logical, therefore, that it could have played a decisive role. For example, it seems obvious that the creation of the Revolutionary Organization 17 November had something to do with the deaths of thirty-four students killed by the police during the occupation of the Polytechnic University in Athens on November 17, 1973— hence the group's name. However, in the cases of Germany, Italy, and Japan, where the fascist regime was over in 1945, why was this episode of history so crucial for the emergence of revolutionary terrorism?

Engene interpreted this finding in terms of legitimacy: "If there are elements of non-democratic periods in the near past, this may contribute to the raising of questions about the true character and legitimacy of the state in the present."[12] But legitimacy is a loose concept, and it is not obvious why legitimacy problems of the past are automatically transmitted to the new regime. Peter Katzenstein offered a more interesting interpretation, based on a comparison of the United States, Germany, Italy, and Japan. On the one hand, politicians of the new regime react with greater fear and harsher repression to the challenge of collective protest, making it easier for terrorist organizations to find recruits and support and to sustain a campaign of violence. On the other hand, terrorists fear the recurrence of authoritarian experiences and intensify the violence of their protest.[13]

There is yet a third explanation, rooted in the literature on comparative politics. Adam Przeworski and his collaborators showed that past instability is a powerful predictor of the survival of the regime.[14] Regimes that have suffered several transitions in the past are less likely to survive. The mechanism is quite simple: People learn from history that the regime can be overthrown and therefore can imagine its demise. Although the Weathermen would not seriously believe that the democratic system could collapse in the United States because of the killings of some police officers, both fascists and revolutionaries in Italy believed that democracy was fragile and could be brought down with some violence. Terrorists tried to end the system because they knew this had happened before. An immediate implication of this hypothesis is that transitions to democracy, when everything is in a state of flux, offer good chances for the emergence of revolutionary terrorism, as can be seen in Greece, Spain, and, to a lesser extent, Portugal.

In a multivariate analysis with the twenty-one countries, the most powerful and robust predictor of the lethality of violence is by far past political instability. It works much better than the size of political mobilization in the '60s or than economic development.[15] Fascist terrorism is also an excellent predictor, but it does not constitute an independent variable. There is an obvious problem of endogeneity in the sense that fascist terrorism could develop in those countries where the extreme left turns violent.

*****

We may conclude, therefore, that whereas revolutionary violent groups emerged in most countries of the developed world in the '70s and '80s, these groups evolved into fully fledged terrorist groups in only a handful of countries; there was a process of political selection. Terrorist groups emerged in countries with past political instability, with powerful social movements in the '60s, with counterproductive repression, and with fascist terrorism.

In principle, the model of political selection could be applied to other forms of domestic terrorism. For instance, a sample of countries with conflicting territorial claims could be built to find the factors that account for the presence of nationalist terrorism in some of these, but not in others. There is ample evidence that in most of them, there were radical groups in favor of violent politics, but only in a few cases did they evolve into lasting and powerful terrorist organizations such as the ETA, the Republican and Loyalist paramilitaries in Northern Ireland, and Hamas and other groups in Palestine.

The whole idea of political selection, however, is problematic in the case of international terrorism. The argument could be applied to terrorist organizations that have a territorial base in a particular country—for example, Palestinian organizations—but it seems much harder for nonterritorial organizations like Al-Qaeda or the anarchist organizations in Europe in the late nineteenth and early twentieth centuries. If the unit of observation is not a country, it is difficult to think of explanatory factors that could answer the question of why some organizations are more successful than others. If contingency plays a significant role in the occurrence of terrorism, there is no doubt that this holds true for international terrorism without a territorial base. In any case, it is worth reminding ourselves that until the emergence of Al-Qaeda, international terrorism represented only a very small fraction of all terrorism.

Endnotes

1. Jan Oskar Engene, *Terrorism in Western Europe: Explaining the Trends since 1950* (Cheltenham, UK: Edward Elgar, 2004).

2. Engene's data set is based on *Keesing's Record of World Events*, whereas my own draws on local sources in each country, including country-based chronologies, data gathered by associations of victims or by the terrorist organizations, local newspapers, official statistics, and many secondary sources. The results are rather different: For instance, Engene reported four fatalities caused by Action Directe in France, but there were in fact twelve.

3. Jorge Torres, *Tupamaros: La derrota de las armas* (Montevideo, Uruguay: Fin de Siglo, 2002), 345–9.

4. Carlos Marighella, *Urban Guerrilla Minimanual* (Vancouver: Pulb Press, 1974).

5. The Quebec Liberation Front, another nationalist group, began its campaign in 1963, but it never became a very dangerous organization.

6. For a comparison between the ETA and the IRA, see Ignacio Sánchez-Cuenca, "Terrorism as War of Attrition: ETA and the IRA" (*Working Paper 204*, Juan March Institute, Madrid, Spain, 2004).

7. Tom Vague, *Anarchy in the UK: The Angry Brigade* (London: AK Press, 1997), 40.

8. See Christopher Hewitt, *Understanding Terrorism in America: From the Klan to Al Qaeda* (London: Routledge, 2003).

9. There was also fascist terrorism in Portugal during the late '70s. Although it is not entirely clear, it seems that the strategy of tension was also attempted in Belgium between 1982 and 1985 (i.e., the Brabant crimes) when a mysterious organization that never claimed their attacks put several bombs in supermarkets, killing almost thirty civilians. See Philip Jenkins, "Strategy of Tension: The Belgian Terrorist Crisis, 1981–1986," *Terrorism* 13 (1990): 299–309.

10. See Peter J. Katzenstein, "Left-Wing Violence and State Response: United States, Germany, Italy and Japan, 1960s–1990s" (working paper, Institute for European Studies, Cornell University, Ithaca, NY, 1998).

11. This is a difficult issue, as France was occupied by a foreign power. Engene, *Terrorism in Western Europe*, includes France among the countries with a discontinuous democratic past.

12. Ibid., 38.

13. Katzenstein, "Left-Wing Violence," 4.

14. Adam Przeworski and others, *Democracy and Development: Political Institutions and Well-Being in the World, 1950–1990* (Cambridge, UK: Cambridge University Press, 2000), 127.

15. No measure of police repression has been included in the analysis for lack of comparable data.

Economic Roots

7

Economic Factors

Ted Robert Gurr

In the aftermath of the U.S. September 11, 2001, attacks, many U.S. officials and observers linked poverty to terrorism. President George W. Bush remarked, "We fight against poverty because hope is an answer to terror."[1] Yet few of the attackers were poor. Muhammad Atta, their leader, was the son of a lawyer and attended graduate school in Germany. Similarly, many Al-Qaeda suspects identified after the attacks were well educated and of middle-class origin. However, they had three other traits in common: (1) most grew up in societies undergoing wrenching socioeconomic changes; (2) their opportunities for political participation were suppressed or sharply restricted by governments; and (3) they were recruited by Islamists committed to jihad against the West.

This chapter surveys some of the complex linkages between economic factors and terrorism, drawing on a report prepared for the Club de Madrid by the Economics Working Group I convened. Group members contributed working papers which provided key inputs for our report and for this chapter. Other scholars' publications also are cited.[2]

Working group members share the assumption that terrorism is a tactic, sometimes a primary strategy, in which armed attacks on civilians are designed to achieve political ends. Terrorism is a choice made by groups waging conflict, not a hard-wired response to deprivation or injustice. The perpetrators justify their decision to use terrorism, rather than other political strategies, by a mix of rational calculation about its costs and benefits plus their ideologically driven pursuit of revolutionary, ethnonational, or religious objectives. Four kinds of connections between economic factors and terrorism are considered here. First, evidence and theory is reviewed about how poverty, relative deprivation, and rapid socioeconomic change can create incentives, or motivations, for people to engage in political violence. Second, two critical intervening variables are examined that shape the political outcomes of these incentives: the political circumstances that dispose militants to use violence and the ideologies used to justify terror. The final topic of discussion is the terrorism-crime nexus, with particular attention to the circumstances in which the objectives of terrorist movements shift from the provision of public, or political, goods to the pursuit of private material benefits.

The analysis is informed throughout by a basic insight from economic—or rational actor—analysis: It is essential to analyze incentives and disincentives that affect militants' decisions to choose terrorist tactics and individual decisions to join, to avoid, or to oppose such groups. As David Gold observed in his working paper for the group, "Economics is not just about whether economic variables can help explain observed outcomes. It is most fundamentally about how human behavior is shaped by the interaction of incentives and constraints."

Poverty, Inequalities, and Socioeconomic Change As Causes of Terrorism

Poverty per se is not a direct cause of terrorism

Macro studies show that terrorism can occur anywhere but is more common in developing societies rather than in the poorest countries or in the developed West and is especially likely to emerge in societies characterized by rapid modernization and lack of political rights.[3] Studies of participants in terrorist organizations demonstrate that militants tend to be better educated and are more likely to be of middle-class background than the populations from which they come. Krueger and Malečková's careful analysis of 1990s data on Hizballah fighters in Lebanon supports this conclusion. Jeroen Gunning said in his working paper for the Economics Working Group that the principle holds whether the terrorist organization in question has ideological or ethnonational motives, religious or secular orientations. Groups as diverse as Hamas, Hizballah, Euzkadi ta Askatasuna (ETA) in the Basque country, the Red Army Faction in Germany, the Tamil Tigers in Sri Lanka, and Al-Qaeda all share this characteristic: that is, organizers and militants are likely to be recruited from the better-educated and more advantaged members of their respective group.

Poverty nonetheless contributes indirectly to the potential for political violence. David Keen has proposed that a country's failure to create a viable economy is one of the root causes of civil war.

Low levels of development create masses of young people with few alternatives—people with essentially zero opportunity costs—who become natural recruits for rebel and terrorist groups.[4] Gunning observed in his working paper that terrorist groups operating from rural areas, such as the Revolutionary Armed Forces of Colombia (FARC), are likely to recruit rank-and-file members from poor and badly educated backgrounds, even if their leaders have more advantaged backgrounds. In their detailed study of the economics of civil war in Congo, Léonce Ndikumana and Kisangani Emizet have documented their argument that in Congo, as elsewhere in Africa, "low-level income and low growth rate reduced the cost of organizing rebellions and also reduced the government's ability to fight a counterinsurgency."[5] This analysis should apply terrorism as well as to rebellion terrorism—all the more so because in Central Africa, as Lyubov Mincheva pointed out in her working paper for the Economics Working Group, rebellions entail a great deal of indiscriminate violence against civilians that would be labeled as terrorism if they occurred elsewhere.

Inequalities are more important than poverty as a source of terrorism

Poverty is seldom invoked by militants to justify their actions. Rather, they claim to act on behalf of groups that are repressed or marginalized by dominant groups. Such claims echo the essential insight of the relative deprivation theory of political violence, which is that people become resentful and disposed to political action when they share a collective perception that they are unjustly deprived of economic and political advantages or opportunities enjoyed by other groups.[6] The groups that support and give rise to terrorist movements usually are relatively disadvantaged because of class, ethnic, or religious cleavages. Terrorism in nineteenth-century Europe took root among marginalized urban workers. In the modern world, as Gunning pointed out in his working paper, "the FARC drew, and continues to draw, much of its support from impoverished peasant farmers in Colombia. The Provisional IRA (Irish Republican Army) was, and is, in part motivated by the socioeconomic marginalization of Catholics in Northern Ireland. The same can be said of Hizballah and the socioeconomic marginalization of the Shi'a in Lebanon, the Tamil Tigers in Sri Lanka, and the Brigate Rosso and the working classes in Italy."

Tore Bjørgo has contended that discrimination on the basis of people's ethnic or religious origin is the chief root cause of ethnonationalist terrorism such as the campaigns of the Provisional IRA in

Northern Ireland, the Tamil Tigers in Sri Lanka, and the Kurdish Workers' Party, known as the PKK, in Turkey. When sizeable minorities are systematically deprived of rights to equal social and economic opportunities or are obstructed from expressing their cultural identities—for example, by being forbidden to write or publish in their language or to practice their religion—this often leads to the rise to self-determination movements. If they are also barred from political access, they are likely to choose violent forms of struggle including terrorism. This is particularly the case, Bjørgo suggested, when the conflict becomes longstanding and bitter, with few prospects for a mutually acceptable solution.[7]

The resentment of inequalities created and maintained by dominant groups helps explain the findings reported by Krueger and Malečková. Public opinion polls taken in 2001 in the West Bank and Gaza showed that the more educated Palestinians are, the more they support armed attacks against civilians inside Israel. From a relative deprivation perspective, we would expect educated Palestinians to be more resentful of their status as an occupied people and thus more supportive of terrorism—especially in a political context where nonviolent political means have been largely closed to them. The authors of this study also noted that a sharp increase occurred in educational attainment of Palestinians in the 1980s, followed by a marked deterioration in their employment prospects.[8] This is consistent with a classic relative deprivation argument: Increasing expectations followed by declining attainments—in the economic or political sphere—create intense grievances and support for political action.

The relative deprivation argument also helps account for the common observation that the leaders of political, ethnic, and sectarian movements usually are better educated and of higher status than most of the population from which they come—something that is true of leaders of almost all political organizations, as Ekkart Zimmermann noted. They are most likely to have had personal experience of class or ethnic or religious barriers to upward mobility and thus have greater incentives to organize political action. But why should terrorism be their strategy of choice? Recall the findings, cited previously, that terrorism is most common in countries with sharply restricted political rights. This means high opportunity costs for conventional political action and relatively lower costs for political violence generally and terrorism specifically. Moreover, in relatively poor countries, as noted already, governments have limited resources to redress grievances or to fight counterinsurgency campaigns.

Rapid socioeconomic change increases the risks of terrorism

Evidence cited previously suggests that terrorism is most common in countries in the middle range of economic development. This is so, the Working Group concluded, because economic change creates conditions conducive for instability and the emergence of militant movements and ideologies, as Mancur Olson pointed out in the 1960s. Different aspects of the growth process have reinforcing effects. One is the likelihood that some groups will gain much more advantage from economic development than others. If inequalities increase along preexisting lines of class or ethnic cleavage, the incentives for revolutionary or separatist movements increase markedly. Another is that large numbers of people are uprooted from traditional life patterns, moving into cities and occupations where they are exposed to discrimination and become susceptible to new ideologies and new forms of political organization.

Some observers emphasize the social trauma that accompanies this process. Rik Coolsaet has argued that terrorism is born not out of religion or poverty but out of marginalization. Anarchist terrorists of the nineteenth century found an audience among the marginalized working classes. Fascists in the 1930s appealed to nationalists but also to people living in the personal uncertainty caused by the Great Depression.[9] Yigal Carmon's comments for the Economics Working Group parallel Coolsaet's interpretation that rapid modernization in the contemporary Islamic world threatens traditional people. Those disoriented by sweeping socioeconomic change are especially susceptible to movements that provide explanations and a program of political action.

Empowerment of women may reduce incentives for terrorism

Although women have occasionally been recruited as suicide bombers—among Palestinians, Sri Lankan Tamils, and Chechens—in general they seldom support terrorism. Cross-national studies show that the higher women's relative educational status and political participation, the less common are political violence and instability.[10] Three causal processes may be at work. First, educated and empowered women may socialize youth in ways that inhibit their susceptibility to recruitment by violent organizations. Second, they may also help strengthen civil society organizations that provide alternatives to political militancy. And third, in the longer run, women's education contributes to declining birth rates, leading to a reduction in the risks posed by large youth populations.

The general conclusion of the Economics Working Group is that structured inequalities within countries—not poverty per se—are breeding grounds for violent political movements in general and terrorism specifically. Rapid socioeconomic change feeds this process. The growth of inequalities across the interdependent global system has similar consequences (see Atanas Gotchev's contribution in this book).

Political Choices of Terrorism

When systematic economic and political inequalities across groups coincide with sharp restrictions on political rights, disadvantaged groups are ripe for recruitment by political movements. Ethnonationalist and revolutionary movements like those of Kosovar militants, Chechen rebels, and Colombia's Marxist FARC usually emerge in the context of larger political conflicts centered on the demands of disadvantaged groups. Militants have choices. They can organize strikes, demonstrations, political agitation, economic boycotts, sabotage, or guerrilla warfare. Their resort to terrorism is often a tactic in a larger campaign that leaders choose and then discard depending on opportunities and costs. A recent study shows that 124 out of 399 terrorist groups are affiliates of, or splits from, political parties. [11]

In what circumstances do political movements shift to terrorist strategies? A general principle cited in working papers by Zimmermann and Michael Stohl, among others, is that semirepressive regimes contribute to the escalation of political conflicts to terrorism by relying on an inconsistent mix of repression and reform. The prospect of reform increases militants' incentives for political action; the regime's use of repression reduces the opportunity costs of oppositional violence, including terrorism; and inconsistency signals regime weakness. Another general principle, mentioned by Alexander Schmid and Joshua Sinai in their working papers, is that some leaders choose terror tactics in expectation that governments will increase repression, leading to a shift in public support from the government to the terrorists' cause. Other, more specific mechanisms are also identified. Radicalization and a wave of terrorist attacks may result when militants capitalize on popular outrage about a specific hostile event—for example the Bloody Sunday massacre by British soldiers in Londonderry in 1972, Ariel Sharon's visit to the Temple Mount/al-Aqsa Mosque in 2000, and the U.S.-led invasion of Iraq in 2003. In other cases radicalization is the result of spillover from conflicts in neighboring states.

Diasporas also may promote terrorist tactics (see Gabriel Sheffer's contribution in this book). Sheffer observes that twenty-seven of the fifty most active contemporary terrorist organizations are either segments of ethnonational or religious diasporas or are supported by them. Members of diasporas of Kurds, Palestinians, Sikhs, Tamils, and many others are motivated by discrimination and repression against kindred in their homelands—and elsewhere—to organize and to support violent resistance. Diaspora activists are "sensitive to the miseries of their brethren in hostlands, homelands, and third or fourth countries of residence," he observed in his working paper for the Economics Working Group. When they see that nonviolent protest is ineffective, "they tend to become more aggressive and form cells and networks for planning and executing violent and terrorist activities." They do not expect to win by such tactics but rather to dramatize injustices and to create imperatives for reform.

The policy challenge is how to reduce the incentives for groups in conflict to choose terrorist tactics and how to increase the incentives to give it up. I have advocated the general principle that democratic rights and institutions give activists incentives to participate in conventional rather than violent politics. Stohl observed that if governments follow strategies of political accommodation in response to terrorist threats, they may not deter active terrorists but are likely to undermine support for them in the larger population—who no longer see a rationale for terrorism. Just as provocative actions by governments can cause a backlash that precipitates terrorism, accommodation by governments can cause a backlash against terrorists.[12]

Ideologies of Terrorism

Ideologies are key to the rise of political terrorism. Radical doctrines profoundly affect how people interpret their situation, respond to efforts to mobilize them, and choose among alternative strategies of political action. Bjørgo observed in his working paper that "the presence of charismatic ideological leaders able to transform widespread grievances and frustrations into a political agenda for violent struggle is a decisive factor behind the emergence of a terrorist movement." Militant and exclusionary ideologies—extreme nationalism, jihadist doctrines, militant Hinduism—all frame disaffected people's ideas about what is possible, permissible, and required. Zimmermann noted that such ideologies can shift cost–reward ratios by convincing people induced into terrorist acts that their sacrifices will have payoffs—if not in this life then in the next.

People whose lives are disrupted by rapid modernization, for example when sudden oil wealth precipitates a change from tribal to high-tech societies in one generation or less, are especially susceptible to radical ideologies. When traditional norms and social patterns become irrelevant, people are ripe for conversion to new ideologies based on religion or nostalgia for a glorious, mythic past. Ideologies derived from Islamic principles are powerful because, for traditional people in Arab societies, religion covers all aspects of life and gives meaning, counsel, and justifications for action. Depending on the content of ideologies and the objectives of those who propagate them, they may create a potential for political violence and terrorism. Rapid political change and insecurity can have similar consequences, for example opening opportunities for protagonists of militant nationalism in East Central Europe in the 1990s.

In a transnational world, ideologies also help members of far-flung groups coordinate action. Ideologies of Palestinian or Kurdish or Chechen nationalism connect dispersed communities in support of a common objective and also facilitate the provision of international support. Similarly, jihadist doctrine helps Islamist militants connect with marginalized people throughout the Muslim world who experience what Coolsaet in his recent book called "a persistent climate of humiliation and oppression."[13]

Ideologies differ in both type and function. They may be used to justify nationalist aspirations, calls for revolution, cultural purification, or a mix of these and other goals. Sheffer and Gunning both pointed out in their working papers that only some Muslim activists are concerned about jihad; others have more limited political and welfare goals. Thus, Islamist doctrine can be used to promote both violent action and provision of welfare goals. Gold noted in his working paper that Hamas has become a successful social service agency, whereas the Taliban first achieved prominence by providing security on trade routes between Afghanistan and Pakistan. He suggested this interpretation: Militant groups that supply local public goods require mechanisms that allow them to control access to the goods and services being supplied. The need to control access helps explain their resort to violence. Participation in violence helps to binds members to the group and makes it difficult for them to leave, thereby providing a solution to the free-rider problem inherent in all production of public goods. In brief, the provision of welfare goods and terrorist action jointly contribute to maintenance of the organization as well as to the long-run pursuit of leaders' political objectives.

Gunning offered an important qualification of the assumption that ideologies determine political action. The content of ideology is in part a product of socioeconomic and political changes. He used Hamas's advocacy of radical solutions as an illustration. Its constituency includes a high percentage of refuges and a significant percentage of highly educated people. Politically, Hamas members have had little trust in the efficacy of those in power in the Palestinian Authority and even less confidence in dialogue with Israel. Its doctrine of violent struggle, including support of suicide operations during the Second Intifada, was a reflection of these traits. The advent of contested elections in the Palestinian Authority and the Israeli withdrawal from Gaza evidently are prompting a shift in Hamas doctrine away from suicide bombing and towards conventional politics. If the argument is correct, Hamas' accession to the power in the Palestinian Authority in Spring 2006 likely will reinforce this shift, though probably without a formal break from Hamas' core ideological commitment to Israel's destruction. The general point, according to Gunning is that, "ideology is not an eternal given; it is molded and re-molded by the life experiences of those inventing, adopting and advocating it."[14]

Alexander Schmid offered one other qualification in his working papers: Ideology is not always necessary for terrorist activity. A collective or individual desire for revenge against acts of repression may be motivation enough. Similarly, he noted that criminal groups like the Colombian drug cartels have engaged in terrorism to prevent extraditions to the United States without any gloss of ideology. Indeed, the terrorism–crime connection is discussed at greater length in the next section.

Financing Terrorism

Under what circumstances do militants shift from using terrorism in pursuit of ethonational, religious, or revolutionary objectives to self-serving material gain? Jessica Stern has quoted a disillusioned jihadist: "Initially I was of the view that [the leaders] were doing jihad, but now I believe that it is a business and people are earning wealth through it...I thought [the leaders] were true Muslims, but now I believe that they are fraud, they are selling Islam as a product...First I was there for jihad, now I am there for my financial reasons."[15] This sharply illustrates one terrorist's agenda shift, motivated by disillusion with corrupt leaders and his own self-interest. The more general question is whether and why leaders and entire movements choose to seek private gain.

A strong argument has been made that rebellions are motivated by greed rather than grievance. Paul Collier and collaborators have interpreted rebellion as an industry that generates profits from looting, especially of primary commodity exports, and have reported econometric models and case studies generally consistent with the theory.[16] The question is whether a similar model could be proposed for political terrorism. If consistent with empirical evidence, this theory would imply a much closer connection between economic conditions and terrorism than the evidence surveyed at the outset of this chapter about the weak and indirect links among poverty, discrimination, and terrorism.

But I doubt that "terrorism as greed" is a sustainable general argument. Leaders of terrorist movements are more plausibly conceived as political entrepreneurs motivated by personal and ideologically driven political ambition. Shared ideology and social pressures motivate most rank-and-file, unless and until they become disillusioned like the jihadist quoted earlier. Schmid cited a study of the recruitment motives reported by violent activists in Kashmir. Of them, approximately one-third were either jobless or classified as opportunists; another third joined out of religious and political conviction or because of attraction to the movement; and a third were responding to peer pressure, persuasion, or threats.[17]

The linkage between terrorism and crime is mainly a functional one. Although political terrorism is often characterized as rebellion on the cheap, it does require resources for arms, logistics, and sustenance and shelter for activists. Consequently, terrorist movements frequently engage in criminal activity to finance their activities, relying on robbery; kidnapping for ransom; extortion; and trafficking in drugs, scarce commodities, or consumer goods. They also may receive funds and arms from diasporas, private sympathizers, and foreign governments. Alternatively, they cooperate or form alliances with preexisting criminal networks. If the proceeds of criminal activity are substantial and secure, they provide incentives for agenda shifts by some militants and in some cases for entire movements.

The Provisional IRA had an estimated $10 million per annum in funding, according to a 1990s study, some of it from abroad but mostly gained from robberies and racketeering as well as extortion and kidnapping, welfare fraud, and running illegal drinking clubs. The IRA also branched out into legitimate businesses including construction firms, shops, and pubs.[18] Some IRA members made their livelihood by such activities; indeed some may have joined to pursue private gains, but the movement as a whole never lost its primary focus on gaining political ascendancy.

The main Colombian Marxist insurgent movement, the FARC, has long had a close relationship with drug cartels that some have labeled narcoterrorism. By most accounts the linkage is a sometime alliance based on interests that may or may not coincide at any given time and place. The FARC's financial basis rests on kidnapping and, especially, extortion of both legal and illicit businesses in areas under its control. In 1977 the "narcos" decided to locate processing facilities in FARC-controlled areas and relied on the guerrillas to maintain order and security in exchange for paying production taxes. Subsequently, however, as the "narcos" developed their own paramilitaries, this marriage of convenience broke down, and paramilitaries fought with guerrillas for local control. The FARC reportedly continues to extract significant revenue from the coca trade but is not directly engaged in growing, processing, or trafficking.[19] The FARC's official position is that drugs should be legalized, yet the organization's financial drug dependence presumably affects leaders' estimates of the costs and benefits of continuing their insurgency despite recurrent government peace initiatives. Bjørgo suggested as a general principle that "leaders or factions within the militant movement sometimes oppose political solutions to the conflict because it would undermine their vested 'business interests.' Why should the Colombian FARC guerrillas seriously support a peace solution when they run a highly successful ransom-for-money business and collect protection taxes from drug barons?"

Algeria's Islamist insurgents offer a contrasting example. In Miriam Lowi's view "a politically motivated insurgency quickly turned into an instrument of predation." At the outset in 1992 the insurgents sought financing through raids and armed robberies but soon shifted to extortion and pillaging of commercial traffic, seizing property, and taxing local populations. Their next step was involvement in the parallel economy and illicit trade in hashish, vehicles, and food products. Algeria has a vast number of unemployed young men, many of whom were attracted to the insurgency by economic opportunity. "As the violence became increasingly articulated with the microeconomy, the interest in capturing the state gave way to looting it and, eventually, to holding the state at bay so as to focus squarely on gaining and maintaining access to resources. Violence and the Islamist insurgency provided a cover for corruption and contraband."[20]

A transnational example comes from the Balkans. Citing the collaboration between the Kosovar ethnonationalists who operate throughout Albanian populated areas in the Balkans on the one hand and the *fares*—the Albanian criminal clan network that smuggles arms, drugs, and people across borders of Kosovo, Albania, and Macedonia on the other hand—Mincheva contended in her working paper that cross-border identity networks and shared ideology are key conditions for the establishment of terrorist–criminal alliances. She noted that transborder ethnonational movements provide the settings in which such linkages develop, though the movements are not directly responsible for the cross-border export of terrorism, nor do they directly engage in cross-border drugs and weapons trafficking. Rather the diffusion of militarized conflict across borders from the movement's more mobilized to less mobilized segments, and worse yet, the new conflict generated in neighboring territory makes political enterpreneurs professional "weekend warriors" and turns criminal clan activities into a weapons supply enterprise for rebels.[21]

In summary, the examples suggest four different kinds of connections between terrorist organizations and economic crime. Economic crime may be strictly functional, as it was for the IRA, with little effect on the IRA's pursuit of its political objectives. The FARC case illustrates how availability of illegal financing may lead to strategic change: in this case, hypothetically, to sustain the insurgency rather than to give up rents. Islamists in Algeria have largely abandoned their revolutionary objectives and have become political bandits. In the Balkans transborder ethnic ties provide the basis for collaboration between militants and international criminal networks. It is speculated that Islamist doctrine similarly facilitates transstate linkages between jihadists and criminals in Central Asia and elsewhere. In these cases political and material incentives become inextricably connected: Today's terrorists probably are tomorrow's traffickers, and vice versa.

International and Domestic Response Strategies

The analyses in this chapter suggest a number of long-term strategies that should reduce the incentives and opportunities for all violent political movements. They are not likely to dissuade currently active groups from using terrorism but in the long run should dry up their support and should channel future grievances into conventional politics.

The first set of recommendations addresses the socioeconomic environments that breed terrorism:

1. The creation of strategies to mitigate the impact of rapid socioeconomic change on vulnerable segments of the population in poorer countries—more specifically, the implementation of international aid and investment policies that help empower groups most directly affected to control or influence the nature and pace of development. It is especially important to promote participation and opportunities for groups left behind in rapid development. Redistribution of new wealth among the population in the form of education and corresponding job opportunities is important. Education without opportunities is an explosive combination. Even more explosive is expansion of traditional Islamic education that provides no skills for participation in modernizing societies but sanctions jihadist resistance to modernization and its agents.
2. The promotion of women's literacy, education, and economic and political participation. Almost everywhere women are

less likely to join or support militant political movements than men and, to the extent they are empowered, can provide a domestic constraint on terrorist recruitment and action.

3. Encouraging governments of heterogeneous societies to reduce group discrimination and barriers to domestic socioeconomic mobility by promoting international norms of equal rights, supporting small-scale private enterprise, and offering inducements such as conditional economic assistance and favorable trading partnerships to governments that implement such policies.

4. Enlisting the cooperation of the private sector in long-run socioeconomic reform efforts, for example by designing investment and employment strategies that help incorporate disadvantaged and marginalized groups. International corporations and investors are in a strong position to influence the policies of governments in host countries in ways that minimize risks of terrorist attacks on their facilities and personnel.

The second set of strategies deals with the political environments that facilitate terrorism, on the principle that political development is an essential complement to socioeconomic improvements:

5. Promoting the growth of the middle and professional classes and their organizations. Middle-class, civil society groups usually have strong incentives to support nonviolent politics and to discourage militants from terrorist actions. Terrorist campaigns have well-documented adverse effects on economic performance.

6. In countries where political militants are active but have not yet resorted to terrorism, encouraging governments to design opportunities—political and economic ones—that alter cost–benefit calculations for political activists in ways that discourage recruitment to and support for terrorism. Promote political compromise with dissident groups, particularly those that have broad-based support. International engagement in such situations should be done in agreement with local governments and social groups; otherwise it may worsen the conflicts.

7. Countering the propagation of extremist ideologies, especially but not only jihadist doctrines, and encouraging the international media, local schools, and public figures to challenge and to provide alternatives to hate propaganda.

Supporting mainstream Islamist scholarship, media, and reform programs. Devising programs that increase Muslims' favorable exposure to Western societies, for example by sponsoring short-term visits of Muslim students to Western communities.

Long-run socioeconomic and political policies to reduce the risks of terrorism are easier to implement in democracies than autocracies. Western-style democracy is not a magic bullet, however. In some societies, transitions to democracy prompt cultural resistance and may create short-term opportunities for violent political movements. International support for specific reforms like those listed above is a first step. Achieving those reforms will contribute over the longer run to the emergence of strong and stable democracies.

It is also important, however, to address the proximate causes of terrorism. The third set of recommendations, therefore, aims to reduce the material and political resources of militant organizations, and calls for the adoption of the following proposals:

8. Interrupting the flow of financial resources to militant groups is already being pursued by the international community but has limited effectiveness because (1) most terrorism is low cost; and (2) militants have recourse to alternative remittance systems, use of couriers, and fund-raising locally through crime. Attempting to cut off all international funds is impossible, and for policies not to be counterproductive, new methods are needed to focus on informal methods. Many charity groups are, first and foremost, engaged in activities whose purposes are to enhance the cultural, civic and economic well-being of their own communities. Thus it is important to allow charities suspected of having funded terrorism to continue helping ordinary people within a system of "robust checks and balances, as exemplified by the approach adopted by the UK Charity Commission" (according to Jeroen Gunning's working paper).

9. Undermining political support for militants may be a more potent strategy. Internationally, diaspora groups—especially those in Western societies—can bring pressure to bear on activists in their homelands to follow more moderate strategies, especially if it can be shown that the alternatives have potential payoffs for reducing their grievances. Domestically, militants always face risks of defection and loss of support from their potential supporters. Offers of amnesty and eco-

nomic incentives to fighters who give up armed struggle have long been used to help defuse rebellions, and are equally applicable to terrorist movements. Governments also should play up the negative consequences of terrorist acts, aiming to delegitimate terrorists in the eyes of their support groups.

10.   Better international coordination and joint action are essential. Regional and international organizations should take the lead in containing cross-border terrorism generated by regional conflicts in the Balkans, Central Africa, the Middle East, and elsewhere, provided this is done in cooperation with the authorities and civil society organizations of countries in each region in conflict. In addition, all governments should create central authorities for international coordination against international terrorism and crime that are capable of taking swift, joint action with counterparts in other countries. The creation and networking of such authorities should help compensate for the fact that judicial and law enforcement systems are still mainly national, whereas borders have become much more porous in ways that facilitate international terrorism and crime.

Endnotes

1.   Quoted in Alan B. Krueger and Jitka Malekčová, "Education, Poverty, Political Violence and Terrorism: Is There a Causal Connection?" *Journal of Economic Perspectives* 17, no. 4 (2004): 119–44.

2.   Working group members are listed below. Their working papers are included in the Club de Madrid's Document Library at http://summit.clubmadrid.org/info/document-library.html.

Alberto Abadie, Harvard University
Jose Antonio Alonso, Universidad Complutense de Madrid
Tore Bjørgo, Norwegian Police University College
Yigal Carmon, Middle East Media Research Institute, USA
Sue Eckert, Brown University
David Gold, New School University, New York
Atanas Gotchev, University of National and World Economy, Bulgaria
Jeroen Gunning, University of Aberystwyth, Wales
Jitka Malečková, Russell Sage Foundation, New York (withdrew)
Lyubov Mincheva, University of Sofia, Bulgaria
Alex Schmid, United Nations Office for the Prevention of International Terrorism (advisory member)
Gabriel Sheffer, Hebrew University of Jerusalem
Joshua Sinai, independent researcher, USA

Michael Stohl, University of California at Santa Barbara
Ekkart Zimmermann, Dresden University of Technology.

3. See Alberto Abadie, "Poverty, Political Freedom, and the Roots of Terrorism" (working paper 10859, *National Bureau of Economic Research*, http://www.nber.org/papers/w10859); and Krueger and Malekčová, "Education, Poverty," 137–41. Other evidence is reviewed in Tore Bjørgo (ed.), *Root Causes of Terrorism: Myths, Realities, and Ways Forward* (London: Routledge, 2005).

4. David Keen, "The Economic Functions of Violence in Civil War" (Adelphi Paper no. 320, International Institute of Strategic Studies, 1998).

5. Léonce Ndikumana and Kisangani F. Emizet, "The Economics of Civil War: The Case of the Democratic Republic of Congo," in *Understanding Civil War: Evidence and Analysis, Volume 1: Africa*, ed. Paul Collier and Nicholas Sambanis (Washington, DC: World Bank, 2005), 63.

6. Ted Robert Gurr, *Why Men Rebel* (Princeton, NJ: Princeton University Press, 1970), chs. 1–5.

7. Bjørgo, *Root Causes*, ch. 20.

8. Krueger and Malekčová, "Education, Poverty," 125–9.

9. Rik Coolsaet, *Al-Qaeda: The Myth. The Root Causes of International Terrorism and How to Tackle Them* (Ghent, Belgium: Academia Press, 2005).

10. See Mary Caprioli, "Primed for Violence: The Role of Gender Inequality in Predicting Internal Conflict," *International Studies Quarterly* 49 (2005): 161–78.

11. Ami Pedahzur and Leonard Weinberg, *Political Parties and Terrorist Groups* (London: Routledge, 2003).

12. See Jeffrey Ian Ross and Gurr, "Why Terrorism Subsides: A Comparative Study of Canada and the United States," *Comparative Politics* 21, no. 4 (1989): 405–26.

13. Coolsaet, *Al-Qaeda*.

14. Quotations are from Jeroen Gunning's working paper for the Economics Working Group. Also see his "Peace with Hamas? The Transforming Potential of Political Participation," *International Affairs* 80, no. 2 (2004): 233–56; and John Tirman and Marianne Heiberg (eds.), *Turning the Tables on Terrorism: Understanding Protracted Conflicts* (Philadelphia: University of Pennsylvania Press, in press).

15. Jessica Stern, *Terror in the Name of God: Why Religious Militants Kill* (New York: Harper Collins, 2003), 213–7.

16. The argument and evidence were first presented in Collier and Anke Hoeffler, "Greed and Grievance in Civil War" (working paper 2355, World Bank Policy Research, Washington, DC, World Bank, 2001). The argument has now been evaluated in a series of comparative case studies in Collier and Sambanis (see note 5). Support for the general argument is qualified at best.

17. Citing Paul Medhurst, *Global Terrorism: A Course Produced by UNITAR* (New York: UNITAR, 2000), 68.
18. John Horgan and Max Taylor, "Playing the 'Green Card'—Financing the Provisional IRA: Part I," *Terrorism and Political Violence* 11, no. 2 (1999): 1–38.
19. Information in this paragraph is drawn from Jennifer S. Holmes, Sheila Amin Gutiérrez de Piñeres, and Kevin M. Curtin, "A Subnational Study of Insurgency: FARC Violence in the 1990s." This text can be viewed at http://usregsec.sdsu.edu/docs/holmes3.
20. Miriam R. Lowi, "Algeria, 1990–2002: Anatomy of a Civil War," in Collier (see note 5), 232–3.
21. These links are explored in Lyubov Mincheva, "Cross-Border Terrorism: Economic and Related Causes" (working paper for the Economics Working Group). They are now the basis for a joint research project with the author of this chapter.

8

Terrorism and Globalization

Atanas Gotchev

Following the September 11, 2001, attacks on the United States and the subsequent war on terrorism, some of the debate focused on the root causes of terrorism and possible response strategies. Part of this debate addressed globalization and whether it provides incentives and facilitates international terrorism. Though no empirical studies provide conclusive evidence that globalization creates terrorism, some of the literature implies that certain aspects of this phenomenon may create incentives for terrorism and suggests that in a globalized world it becomes much easier to organize, to finance, and to sustain terrorist tactics and activities. The purpose of this contribution is to explain the dynamics behind the relationship between terrorism and globalization and to show how some of its malign effects could be addressed.

Over the past twenty-five years, globalization has been a hotly debated phenomenon. Most commonly, it is associated with the development of global production and markets and their social, political, and cultural consequences. The majority of analyses take an economic perspective and associate it with increased economic integration, growth of international exchange, and interdependence.[1] From this perspective, globalization implies liberalization—that is, the elimination of state restrictions on trade and foreign exchange as well as the reduction of controls on movements of capital, labor, knowledge, and technology. Globalization is, however, also regarded as a phenomenon brought about by technological and social change, furthering the links of human activities across regions and continents.[2]

The globalization discourse cuts across the ideological spectrum and academic disciplines. It is very heated, contentious, and polarized. Proponents of globalization regard it as a panacea, promoting economic growth and prosperity and spreading the values of democracy, restricting governmental interference in the international economy, and enhancing the ease with which labor, ideas, capital, technology, and profits can move across borders. The defenders of globalization also argue that it has provided opportunities for enormous economic and social benefits, particularly for countries that have managed to use the opportunities provided by global markets.

Opponents of globalization regard it as a thoroughly negative process, increasing the domination and control of developed nations of the poor and less developed ones. As observed by Douglas Kellner, for critics globalization is a cover for global capitalism and imperialism and is condemned as another form of imposition of the logic of capital and the market on more regions of the world.[3] For instance, James Petras and Henry Veltmeyer contended that "although globalization is presented as an *economic* process, a paradigm for describing and explaining worldwide trends, it is better viewed as a *political* project, a desired outcome that reflects the interplay of specific socio-economic interests."[4] They argued that globalization provides an inadequate description and understanding of worldwide trends and that the concept of imperialism is more suitable in this regard. From this perspective, globalization can be regarded as a new form of imperialism, suggesting power struggles, the domination of the stronger, and—therefore—a sequence of conflicts.

This brief outline of the opposing perspectives demonstrates that globalization has to be regarded as a complex and contradictory process with positive and negative attributes. According to the advocates of globalization, interdependence should result in a dynamic and constantly modernizing world of prosperous nations.[5] However, it must be taken into account that integration in the world economy has been uneven, with the effects of globalization differing from nation to nation. The consequences of globalization are mainly positive for the developed countries of the West and the newly industrialized nations—the so-called true globalizers—and largely negative for the weak globalizers from the less developed world.

A World Bank study on globalization, growth, and poverty suggested that weak globalizers increasingly diverge from the global econonomic decline.[6] In the context of the global economy, such countries tend to be economically marginalized. Weak globalizers become less competitive, incomes fall or stagnate, absolute poverty grows, social stratification increases, and—in many cases—life expectancy declines. The social consequences are unemployment, political tension, and the growth of religious fundamentalism. Large strata of the population in such countries regard globalization as imposed from the hegemonic capitalist countries and international financial institution. This, indirectly, creates an environment that can facilitate violent behavior and acts of terrorism.

The group of weak globalizers largely comprises African and Muslim countries, some of which have been strongly associated with terrorism. In fact, as Edward Gresser noted, most of the Muslim countries were steadily deglobalized over the last twenty-five years. Unlike East Asia, the growing share of young people, especially men, in relation to the overall population—the demographic bulge—and urbanization in the Muslim world have been accompanied by shrinking shares in world trade and investment. In 1980, about 13.5 percent of world exports came from these countries, whereas in 2002 the figure was about 4 percent. In 2001 the Muslim world—with a population of 1.3 billion people—received barely as much foreign direct investment as Sweden, a country with a population of nine million people. Deglobalization made many Muslim countries poorer—the per capita gross domestic product of Arab countries, for instance, has shrunk by nearly 25 percent since 1980, falling from $2,300 to $1,650.[7]

Though the review of the globalization debate presented here is far from comprehensive, it suggests that globalization has resulted in uneven development and inequitable distribution of the positive effects of globalization across countries. As noted by Veltmeyer, Robert Kapstein, then director of the Council on Foreign Relations, pointed out as early as 1996 that neoliberal capitalism bears a tendency toward excessive social inequalities in the distribution of global resources and income. This, he continued, led to "social discontent the forces of which could be mobilized politically in ways that are destabilizing for the democratic regimes and the system as a whole."[8] The deepening division between true and weak globalizers in the 2000s can thus be seen as creating a permissive environment for terrorism. This environment includes both incentives and opportunities to organize, finance, and carry out terrorist acts.

Globalization As a Cause and Motivation for Terrorist Activities

Globalization has increased inequalities and social polarization within and between nations. Although different studies fail to provide conclusive evidence that poverty and inequality are directly linked to terrorism, it is evident that economic deprivation increases the demands for political change. Economic disparities usually lead to political upheavals and could invite interested groups to resort to terrorism as a method of achieving the desired goals. As Tore Bjørgo noted, poverty has frequently been used as justification for violence by social revolutionary terrorists, who claim to represent the poor and marginalized strata without being poor themselves.[9] Such terrorism is more commonly associated with countries with a medium level of development and whose societies are characterized by rapid modernization and transition (see Ted Robert Gurr's contribution in this book).

The current unequal status quo of wealth and capital accumulation in developed countries could provoke waves of terrorist acts justified by the cause for fairer distribution of global wealth. The 2000–2001 World Bank Development Report indicated that 2.8 billion of the world's six billion people are living on less than two dollars a day with limited access to education and health care and lack of political power and voice, leaving them therefore extremely vulnerable to ill health, economic dislocation, personal violence, and natural disasters.[10] Sustaining this world order only by means of military power and without long-term efficient developmental strategies is bound to provoke resistance. Militant groups could justify terrorism as a last resort, excusing it as a tactical response of the weak. In other words, the cause of a just distribution of global wealth may become one of the contributing factors for cycles of asymmetrical warfare against the richer countries and their allies.

The United Nations has recognized the importance of addressing the issues of poverty and terrorism in a comprehensive way. The aftermath of the September 11 attacks and the subsequent war against terrorism suggest that confronting terrorism only with military force, while failing to deal with the issues of poverty and inequality, is bound to create weak client regimes that are unable to withstand the pressures of globalization. Such states cannot apply the principles of good governance, they experience poverty and instability, which leads to opposition and violence and thus creates the breeding ground for terrorism.

Globalization, however, also fosters political and cultural resistance. The development of global markets for goods, services, and capital compels societies to alter their cultural practices. Globalization brings about cultural Westernization and destroys traditional ways of life. In response, this provokes opposition of broad segments in the affected societies, providing another justification for terrorism.[11] Indeed, the infiltration of a supposedly alien and corrupt culture is used by nationalist and radical religious movements as a way of explaining their campaigns. They claim that their violence has the purpose of cleansing their societies and culture from foreign influence. In reality, these are often mere excuses, yet it is also true that the "threat to the local way of life" has become a convenient motivation and justification for terrorist activities.[12]

Globalization and the Development of New Minorities

There are, however, even more tangible ways that globalization has created conditions in which terrorism can flourish. Wage differentials, differences in career opportunities, and the provision of public services across countries coupled with the availability of global transportation and communication networks have brought about unprecedented global migration to countries which provide better opportunities in terms of human development. This has led to the development of new minorities in settled societies, many of which are linked to kindred groups elsewhere. A similar process occurred in the 1960s and 1970s when as a result of decolonization new minority groups appeared in countries like France and Britain. Because of differentials in incomes and standards of living, migration streams from the less developed world flow toward not only the most developed industrial countries but also the emerging market economies and to medium-income countries in Central, Eastern, and Southern Europe. Moreover, processes of migration also occur among the less developed countries and in the Arab world—for instance, from Iraq to Jordan or from Egypt to Jordan.

This process and its implications can be illustrated by looking at the Bulgarian border statistics for the years 2002 and 2003. This data indicate that the difference between recorded arrivals and departures is approximately 300,000 people annually. One of the assumptions is that a large percentage of these people stay in Bulgaria in an effort to explore opportunities for moving further west into the enlarged European Union (EU) zone. Indeed, a similar situation can be observed in other EU accession countries, such as Romania. The issue of concern is that, for a country like Bulgaria with a population of around eight million, the figure is substantial. If one assumes that all of the illegal immigrants stay in Bulgaria, then the size of this new community may soon become equal to that of the Roma minority in Bulgaria.

Segments of these minorities participate in criminal activities, and this can help to facilitate terrorism, especially since the distinction between *political* and *criminal* is becoming increasingly blurred. As Lyubov Mincheva observed, the Serbian criminal mafia, the Albanian drug mafia, and Bosnian Muslims terrorists frequently act in concert and engage in "marriages of convenience" not to promote Wahhabism but to pursue their shared interest in making money. Likewise, criminal groups like the Colombian drug cartels have engaged in terrorism to prevent extradition to the United States without any gloss of ideology. Such malign connections are evident not only in the Balkans but also in the Caucuses and in Latin America. These linkages often arise from what could be described as the political economy of conflict. Even if the initial motivation of militant groups to turn to crime was to finance their political activities, over time politics tends to become a mere excuse for crime for profit. Bjørgo points out that leaders or factions within militant movements sometimes oppose political solutions to conflict because this would undermine their vested business interests. Why should there be a political solution of the Transnistrian conflict in Moldova or of the conflicts in the Caucuses, when the opposing parties can take advantage of smuggling alcohol, tobacco, consumer goods, weapons, and drugs and can seize the opportunity that exists simply because the area of the conflict is out of the control of tax and customs authorities?[13]

More specifically, the involvement of the new minorities in these networks could be said to facilitate international terrorism in three related ways. First, it improves terrorists' logistical support. Organized crime and terrorist groups frequently use similar—sometimes the same—means and routes for moving materials, people, and funds across boundaries. The so-called Informal Value Transfer Systems (i.e., underground banking networks) were originally designed to serve the needs of minority groups who wanted to send to or receive funds from their families. The improved versions of such systems, however, were developed by criminal groups and are now also used by terrorist groups.

Second, new minorities provide additional sources of funding. Some of the proceeds originating from the illegal businesses of members of the new minorities end up funding terrorist groups. These can be either payments for protection and taxes imposed by terrorists, a good will gesture of prosperous members of the community, or a split of profits of a joint criminal–terrorist operation. It should be noted that it is not only illegal businesses that secure funds. Legitimate business operations run by new minority groups—usually small and medium-sized businesses—could also be tracked as sponsors of terrorism.[14] Furthermore, in many developed countries, new minority groups have established cultural institutions, which operate as charities and have been implicated in the donation of millions of dollars to various terrorist organizations.[15] The significance of the different funding schemes in which new minority groups are involved varies, and not all of them are a major funding source of terrorism. However, this type of funding is an important enabler of terrorist activities, as it diversifies funding and makes it more difficult to track. Last but not least, it should be pointed out that even relatively small amounts—for instance, earned in single smuggling or a legitimate business operation—can be used to cause disproportionate damage.

Third, new minorities are a source of human capital for international terrorism. In Sheffer's contribution in this book, he points out that twenty-seven of the fifty most active terrorist organizations today are either segments of ethnonational or religious diasporas or are supported by them. Minorities' attraction to participate in terrorism may result from ideological or religious sentiments. On the other hand, terrorist organizations actively recruit members of minority communities who reside in the industrialized world, particularly in their Western host countries. From the terrorists' perspective, the minorities' education, training, and living experience in the West increases the chances for success in carrying out a terrorist act, especially compared to a terrorist who is residing in a less developed part of the world.

Globalization and the Power of the Nation State

Another aspect worthy of consideration is the consequences of globalization for the nation state. The debate about the fate of the nation state is highly polarized and draws on various changes in governance that may accompany the processes of globalization. Diverging views range from the position that globalization has eliminated state sovereignty or—at best—diminished it in favor of global corporate power to the position that globalization has not undermined statehood at all. A different, and perhaps more promising, approach is to focus not so much on the power of contemporary states but rather on how its functions have changed.

There can be no doubt, for example, that as a result of globalization governments have experienced a decline in their capacity to control their economies. In the 1990s and early 2000s, the volatility of global foreign exchange markets has triggered waves of financial crises affecting even the developed economies of Britain, Italy, and Sweden. In less developed countries, the diminished power of the state to control the economy has led to governmental collapse and state failure. In postcommunist countries, the spin-off effects of the transition toward democratization, economic restructuring, and reintegration in the global economy have weakened the economic and political control of the state, resulting in the failure of law enforcement and the growth of crime as well as deepening income stratification. Furthermore, the fact that international financial institutions grant financial support based on a number of conditionalities also restrict policy options of beneficiary governments. Taking into account that developed countries dominate these institutions, foreign aid policies based on neoliberal recipes and unpopular austerity measures, implemented by beneficiary governments, have provoked popular protests and have led to different forms of mobilization, particularly in the less developed world. The diminished capacity of the less developed countries to control their economies, the weakened capacity of law enforcement, the imposition of Western market values and institutions through the programs of the international financial institutions and other donors are phenomena, at least in part associated with globalization. Although these phenomena should not be regarded as a prime factor, they have provided justifications for extremist movements to resort to violence as a tactical weapon.

The growth of nonstate actors is another argument used to explain the diminished role of the state in the era of globalization. This process has a wide range of implications, both related to the functioning of the international system and state governance. One of these is that the increasing prominence of the nonstate sector has created opportunities for terrorist organizations to avoid direct links with the state and, in particular, with states sponsoring terrorism. Terrorist groups have increasingly begun to rely on amorphous supporters and financial sources. One of the consequences, as pointed out by Matthew Morgan, is that when terrorists do not rely on direct state sponsorship, they become less accountable and harder to track. At the same time, states sponsoring terrorism exercise less control over and have less of an interest in maintaining comprehensive intelligence on radical terrorist organizations.[16] This outcome of globalization makes contemporary international terrorism more difficult to monitor and to predict and limits the utility of traditional political and diplomatic instruments, which cannot be applied effectively against elusive and obscure nonstate actors.

Moreover, though the spread of new technologies has produced considerable benefits in terms of productivity growth, it has also increased the destructiveness and effectiveness of weapons. In turn, global trade and transportation have proliferated new weapons and have made them more readily accessible. As a result, globalization has provided new opportunities for terrorist organizations to acquire and to use more efficient and deadlier weapons and to perform more spectacular and destructive terrorist acts. It has also benefited terrorist groups in terms of targeting.[17] Faster travel and better communication technologies facilitate the operations of terrorist groups and also make it easier to spread radical ideas that may inflame large constituencies. This assists terrorists in fund-raising, in recruiting followers, and in mobilizing support for terrorist groups. At the same time, the sinews of globalization—from pipelines and electricity grids to nuclear power plants and communication networks—provide a range of soft targets for international terrorism.

Finally, globalization has caused changes in the organizational behavior structures of terrorist organizations. The global operations of transnational corporations have provided a good example to terrorist groups for how to plan, to organize, and to accomplish their objectives at the international level. Much like these corporations, terrorist groups have evolved organizationally. As pointed out by Morgan, terrorist groups have moved from strict hierarchical, or vertical, structures to more horizontal and more flexible organizational arrangements.[18] The capacity to adapt to changes copied from the best practice models of transnational corporations has allowed a number of terrorist groups to recruit supporters, to secure funds, and to conceal operations in spite of global efforts to curb terrorist activities.

Response Strategies

There is no easy answer to the question of what our response should be to the developments caused by globalization. Globalization is only one of many factors that influence the development of terrorism. Indeed, as highlighted throughout this book, terrorism is a complex, multifaceted phenomenon and obviously requires a comprehensive and consistent response strategy. To be effective, such a strategy needs to be based on a wide international consensus, including the definition of terrorism, both academic and legal; appropriate antiterrorist policies, strategies, and tactics; as well as the methods of their implementation. Response strategies also require a comprehensive coordination of multilateral, bilateral, and national efforts.

Any attempt to design antiglobalization measures is unrealistic and likely to fail. At the same time, policies to mitigate some of the downside effects of globalization may restrict the base of terrorism in terms of motivation and justification of terrorist activities. These are long-term developmental strategies, which do not aim at the eradication of terrorism but at developing a social and economic environment that will discredit terrorism as a means to achieve political ends. In this respect, strategies to reintegrate weak globalizers into the world economy are an important part of the long-term developmental response to terrorism. Such strategies are likely to curb grievances arising from global inequalities, to decrease anti-Western sentiments, and to curb religious fundamentalism. Moreover, although the integration in the global economy is a process that can be controlled by governments only to a limited extent, multilateral efforts by industrialized countries may facilitate the access of weak globalizers to world markets. For example, developing a duty-free regime for their products and facilitating their membership in international trade organizations is one of the possible approaches. This could be accompanied by subsidized transfer of key inputs and technologies.[19]

Cragin and Chalk pointed out that the success of developmental policies in countering terrorism is strongly related to the type of projects and the mode of implementation. They are correct in saying that underfunded and poorly executed developmental projects could "act as a double-edged sword by precipitating a revolution of rising (and unfulfilled) expectations."[20] This observation can be confirmed by the experience of developmental projects in countries in transition. There is abundant evidence indicating that inappropriately designed projects aimed at alleviating the situation of minority and underprivileged groups in transition economies lead to higher levels of discontent and tension once the funding is exhausted. Such projects tend to be perceived by the beneficiaries as a permanent solution, giving rise to unjustified expectations for a quick and long-lasting improvement. Developmental projects should therefore have the appropriate level of funding commitment, and the projects should be sustained for a relatively long period of time. Governments willing to implement developmental projects should be encouraged and should receive appropriate technical assistance and positive inducements, such as conditional economic assistance. However, economic incentives and conditionalities need to be linked very carefully to avoid possible anti-Western sentiments.

Bjørgo points out that education and related opportunities are an important element in changing the socioeconomic environments that breed terrorism.[21] It is important to consider, however, that different age groups respond to education differently, and it is therefore important to tailor these initiatives carefully. For example, educational programs targeting early age education (i.e., preschool and primary school) tend to be more effective in the longer run. Experience suggests that stronger and more sustainable long-term impacts are achieved if early age education is coupled with women's education and empowerment (see Ted Robert Gurr's contribution in this book). This can be one of the possible approaches to counter the expansion of extremist fundamentalist ideologies.

A number of short-term and coercive measures should be taken. Curbing terrorist financing, for example, could be more efficient if there is a coordinated effort to fight both terrorism and organized crime. Since terrorism and organized crime develop linkages which help them resist international action, it is necessary to design and coordinate strategies aimed at both terrorism and crime. Though international cooperation in the fight against crime has a long history, international cooperation against terrorism is still in its nascent stage. The creation of a new international regime, for instance, should aim to compensate for the situation that judicial and law enforcement systems are national, whereas terrorism and crime are increasingly internationalized. The effort to restrict the funding sources of terrorism should also consider enhanced border and customs controls aimed at restricting illegal transfers of weapons, drugs, and people, particularly in cases in which transfers originate from destinations suspected to have linkages with terrorist groups. These have to be complemented by the development of more sophisticated mechanisms aimed at preventing money laundering. Although difficult to accomplish, serious attention should be given to money transfers by couriers and informal value transfer systems. Furthermore, there are strong indications that some terrorist groups use charities as an important funding source. A system of enhanced control of such activities, while guaranteeing the freedom of such organizations to attain their charitable missions, should be developed. Finally, although terrorism has evolved and relies less on open state sponsorship, it is premature to regard state sponsored terrorism as an unimportant factor. Better international coordination and joint action are essential for constraining this type of terrorism.

Endnotes

1. See Robert Keohane and Joseph Nye, "Globalization: What's New and What's Not? (and So What?)," *Foreign Policy* 118, no. 2 (2000), pp. 104-119.

2. See, for example, Keohane, "The Globalization of Informal Violence, Theories of World Politics, and the 'Liberalism of Fear,'" *International Organization* 52, no. 1 (2002): 29–30. Jan Aart Scholte argued that the ideational and material drivers of globalization are codetermining and that globalization can be explained with reference to trends in production, governance, identity, and knowledge. See Scholte, *Globalization: A Critical Introduction* (Basingstoke: Palgrave Macmillan, 2005), esp. pp. 20–2, and ch. 4.

3. Douglas Kellner, Globalization, Terrorism and Democracy: 9/11 and Its Aftermath in http://www.gseis.ucla.edu/faculty/kellner/essays/globalizationterroraftermath.pdf.

4. James Petras and Henry Veltmeyer, "World Development: Globalization or Imperialism?" in *Globalization and Antiglobalization: Dynamics of Change in the New World Order*, ed. Henry Velt-

meyer (Hants, UK and Burlington, VT, USA: Ashgate Publishing, 2004), 11.

5. Ibid., 23.

6. See David Dollar and Paul Collier, Globalization, Growth, and Poverty: Building an Inclusive World Economy, A World Bank Policy Research Report. A co-publication of the World Bank and Oxford University Press (Washington, DC: World Bank, 2002), esp. the overview (pp. 3-18) and ch. 1 (pp. 31-53).

7. See Edward Gresser, "Blank Spot on the Map—How Trade Policy Is Working against the War on Terror," Progressive Policy Institute Policy Report, February 2003, 1.

8. See Veltmeyer, "The Antinomies of Antiglobalization," in Veltmeyer (see note 4), 171.

9. See Tore Bjørgo, Root Causes of Terrorism: Findings from an International Expert Meeting in Oslo, Norwegian Institute of International Affairs, http://www.nupi.no/IPS/filestore/Root_Causes_report.pdf.

10. See World Bank, World Development Report 2000–2001: Attacking Poverty (New York: Oxford University Press, 2001).

11. See Dani Roderik, Has Globalization Gone too Far? (Washington, DC: Institute for International Economics, 1997), 1; see also Scholte, Globalization, 26.

12. Diverse political movements such as hard-core communists in Russia and Islamic fundamentalists in Turkey can display striking commonalities rooted in a backlash against globalization, see Roderik, Has Globalization Gone too Far, 1. Scholte asserted that micronationalist and religious revivals—encouraged in part by globalization—have promoted a substantial rise in intrastate warfare outside the North, such as in Afghanistan, Angola, Indonesia, Russia, and the former Yugoslavia. See Scholte, Globalization, 283.

13. This paragraph is based on discussions, Working Group on the Economic Causes of Terrorism, International Summit on Democracy, Terrorism, and Security (hereafter referred to as Working Group), Madrid, Spain, March 2005.

14. Matthew Levitt, "Blood Money," Wall Street Journal, June 4, 2003.

15. See, for instance, U.S. General Accounting Office, Terrorist Financing, GAO-04-15, November 2003; and Levitt, "The Political Economy of Middle East Terrorism," Middle East Review of International Affairs Journal 6, no. 4 (2002), pp. 49-65.

16. This and the following two paragraphs draw on Matthew Morgan's analysis. See Matthew J. Morgan, "The Origins of the New Terrorism," Parameters 34, no. 1 (2004): 37.

17. Ibid, 38. See also Paul R. Pillar, "Terrorism Goes Global: Extremist Groups Extend their Reach Worldwide," The Brookings Review, 19 (Fall 2001), 34-37.

18. Ibid, 38.

19. Discussions, Working Group. See also *Addressing the Causes of Terrorism: The Club de Madrid Series on democracy and Terrorism*, Volume 1, pp 24-25, http://www.safe-democracy. org/docs/CdM-Series-on-Terrorism-Vol-1.pdf.
20. Kim Cragin and Peter Chalk, *Terrorism and Development—Using Social and Economic Development to Inhibit Resurgence of Terrorism* (Washington, DC: RAND, 2003), 33.
21. Discussions, Working Group.

9

Diasporas and Terrorism

Gabriel Sheffer

Like most minorities' members and leaders, individuals belonging to internationally dispersed groups and movements—namely, to diasporas—such as Al-Qaeda, Hezbollah, Basque Fatherland and Liberty (ETA), Hamas, and the Liberation Tigers of Tamil Elam (LTTE), vehemently reject their characterization as terrorists and of their violent actions as terrorism. They claim that in view of their pure motivations and noble and highly justified goals they should be considered as freedom fighters; cultural, political, and civil rights activists; protectors of their religions; or anticolonialists and antiglobalizationists. Yet most of these entities' violent activities fit widely accepted views of terrorism and some of its definitions.[1]

Insufficient attention has been given to the differentiated involvement of the various categories of "others," and particularly of diasporans, in the execution of extreme acts of violence and terrorist attacks. In most studies and evaluations, all these groups are lumped together, with no sufficient theoretical, analytical, or empirical distinctions of their varied origins, connections, motivations, capabilities, resources, and contributions to the exacerbation of the conflicts in which they are engaged and to the nature of their related violent or terrorist acts. Thus, there is a need for comparative studies and analyses of the diverse purposes, involvement, and roles of members of such groups and their organizations in violent and terrorist campaigns. This contribution, therefore, offers a classification of these others; it focuses on the motivational, organizational, and behavioral differences among the various entities that use radical violent strategies and tactics; it assesses the degree of the intensity of the use of violence by the various types of others both in their countries of residence and in their perceived or actual homelands; and, finally, it offers some policy-oriented proposals.

A Short Review of Others

It needs to be stressed that diasporic terrorism is not a postmodern phenomenon primarily related to the breakdown of the cold war regime, the so-called weakening of the nation state, the expansion of economic and cultural globalization, the spread of, or distance shrinking, communication technologies, or the increase in global migration.[2] Even a brief and cursory historical review shows that the phenomenon of diaspora support for terrorism has existed as long as modern terrorism and that more fundamental causes should be explored.[3] Indeed, one of the most significant common feature of the various perpetrators and supporters of terrorism—new and old—is that they are others in their hostlands. They are, however, not all the same. Indeed, it is useful to differentiate among the various types these entities represent.

The rapidly growing antiglobalization movement—which during the last decade has been gathering momentum and has proved willing and capable to launch and execute both violent and peaceful protests, demonstrations, and resistance to police forces—is mainly composed of tourists rather than of permanently settled diasporans. Usually, after participating in violent and nonviolent activities such as those in Seattle, Genoa, and Durban, they return to their countries of origin or move to other host countries to launch protests there. Likewise, some of the most blatant terrorist attacks launched by diasporans are executed by hard-core terrorists who reside in other countries and come and leave the host country where they either accomplish, or fail at, their missions. The wish to prevent these acts has been the main driver behind the introduction of radical changes in visa granting and border control in many countries.

The second group is composed of refugees and asylum seekers. According to the United Nations High Commissioner for Refugees (UNCHR), more than twenty million people fall into these categories. Whereas twelve million qualify as refugees, the remaining nine million are asylum seekers and returnees to their homelands that have not been fully reintegrated into their original societies. Also, the majority are internally displaced persons, which makes it inappropriate to regard them as diasporans. According to the UNCHR, the main countries hosting refugees fleeing from difficulties in their homelands are Burundi, Sudan, Somalia, Angola, Sierra Leone, Eritrea, Congo,

Liberia, Rwanda, Lebanon, and Jordan; all are countries that have recently experienced internal turmoil, insurgency, or terrorism.[4]

The third category contains legal and illegal, nonorganized, newly arrived migrants—mostly guest workers or students. Though most, but not all, host countries record the numbers and identities of newly arrived legal migrants, which globally number tens of millions, by definition no reliable figures exist about illegal migrants. Attractive political, economic, and educational conditions lead most of these migrants to try to enter developed and mostly democratic countries, including Australia and Japan. Following the attacks on September 11, 2001, in the United States, most host countries have attempted to limit and control the flow of migrants to prevent both terrorism and worsened economic conditions. Nevertheless, most borders, especially in the European Union and the United States, are porous, and such traffic can hardly be controlled entirely. In this respect, of course, democratic and democratizing states are disadvantaged, as they encounter immense ideological, legal, and practical inhibitions when handling immigration. As a result, many terrorist activities have been carried out by this category of people in more developed democratic states.

Fourth, there are members of organized transstate ethnonational diasporas. These are dispersed persons in various hostlands. The members of these entities are of the same ethnic and national origins, permanently residing in their host countries, and are integrated but not assimilated into their host societies. Core members of these groups are organized and maintain contacts with their homelands. According to current estimates, there are more than 300 million such people worldwide.[5] Some of these organized diasporas are historical, veteran, and established; the Jewish, Armenian, Greek, Indian, and Chinese are obvious examples. Some are relatively new and were established in the nineteenth and early twentieth centuries—for instance, the Italians, Irish, and Polish. Some are incipient diasporas—that is, entities in the early stages of formation and organization—such as the post-1948 Palestinian dispersion, the Russians in the former Soviet Union empire, and the Chechens. Members of both established and incipient diasporas have supported violent and terrorist activities in either their homelands, host countries, or third and fourth countries. Therefore, special attention should be paid to these entities, which is why this contribution focuses on this category.

The final category could be labeled as cultural and religious transnational dispersals. As in the fourth category, these are dispersed groups residing out of their homelands. They share the same beliefs, yet each of them is composed of persons from different ethnic and national backgrounds. Examples of these dispersals are the Muslim, African, and Latino diasporas. As a result of terrorist activities launched by Al-Qaeda and other dispersed Sunni and Shiite Muslim transnational groups and organizations, observers have referred to these groups as homogeneous diasporas. In reality, though, the latest wave of terrorism and other violent actions has been carried out not by highly organized and homogeneous Muslim or North African diasporas but rather—separately and autonomously—by members of older organized and incipient transstate ethnonational diasporas, whose members' only common characteristic is that their religion is Islam. Indeed, much closer attention should be paid to the motivations and purposes of various Muslim, Latino, and African groups, whose origins are in different nation states.

Generally, it is extremely difficult to attribute exact numbers of terrorist activities to each of these categories of others. This is for several reasons:

1. Lack of accurate data
2. The sensitive situation of guest workers and other legal and illegal migrants in their host countries
3. The secrecy surrounding the preventive and secret intelligence activities of various governments
4. The uncertain assimilation and integration rates of such groups that in turn determine the size and influence of the core members in each diaspora.

Yet based on reliable estimates, it is possible to approximately rank these groups according to the intensity and rates of their participation in terrorism. Tourists and refugees are increasingly involved in terrorist activities. At the same time, there is almost no doubt that most of those who carry out terrorist activities are members of transstate ethnonational diasporas and of transnational religious dispersals. A recent study claims that 32.3 percent of all acts of mass casualty terrorism (MCT)—which over the past decade have caused about 1,670 deaths—have been performed by members of what might be called pure ethnonational groups, that is, groups whose most prevalent common characteristic is their belonging to the same ethnic nation; 23.5 percent of MCT—amounting to 5,000 deaths, including September 11—have been performed by so-called pure religious groups, that is to say, people whose group membership is determined by their religious beliefs; and 14.7 percent of MCT—835 deaths—have been performed by mixed ethnoreligious groups, for example, Sunnis or Protestants.[6]

Currently, twenty-five groups have been involved in conflicts or rebellions in either their homelands or host countries, which have espoused terrorism. All these groups have been linked to transstate ethnonational diasporas, and all have performed terrorist acts in addition to their involvement in nonviolent tactical activities, such as propaganda campaigns and legal protest marches and demonstrations.[7] Furthermore, of the fifty most active terrorist organizations and groups, twenty-seven either constitute segments of ethnonational diasporas or are supported by them.[8] Insurgents in Egypt, India (i.e., in the Punjab and Kashmir), Indonesia (i.e., Aceh), Azerbaijan, Sri Lanka, Ireland, Kosovo, Lebanon, Palestine, Israel, Pakistan, Algeria, Turkish Kurdistan, Iraqi Kurdistan, Iran, Greece, the Philippines, and Russia all have received various kinds of support—whether financial, political, diplomatic, or psychological—from their respective diasporic communities.

Among the organizations using terrorism that have proven links to ethnonational diasporic entities are the Palestinian Hamas, Islamic Jihad, and Fatah-Tanzim; the Lebanese Hezbollah; the Egyptian Islamic Jihad and Islamic Group; the Irish Republican Army; the Algerian Armed Islamic Group (GIA); the Indian Barbar Khalsa International; the Sri Lankan LTTE; the Turkish Kurdistan Workers' Party (PKK); and Al-Qaeda, who is connected to and cooperates with various ethnic–religious diasporas.[9]

Regarding the state sponsors of terrorism—according to the United States State Department, these are Saudi Arabia, Iran, Iraq, Syria, Libya, Cuba, North Korea, and Sudan—some of these not only supported activities of their own diasporans in host countries but also supported various types of subversive actions carried out by persons of other nationalities and ethnoreligious backgrounds who are temporary or permanent residents in host countries. It is true that some of the aforementioned governments stopped doing so—the cases of Iraq and Libya are pertinent here—and others have declared that they had taken steps to cooperate in the global campaign against terrorism, such as Iran, Syria, and North Korea. Apparently, however, these latter states, and probably also Sudan, have persisted with the very actions that had led international organizations, other national governments, and academic analysts to regard them as state sponsors of terrorism.

Distinctions and Debates

Although certain similarities exist between the various diasporas and their organizations that use violence and terrorism, three essential distinctions must be made between them.

The first distinction, which has already been mentioned, is between terrorist actions carried out by pure ethnonationalists who pursue nationalist goals in their homelands or host countries and pure religionists who aim to achieve religious objectives. This distinction is essential for understanding current terrorism and, more particularly, for accurately grasping diasporas' varying motivations for employing such violence.[10] This, however, is far from simple. For example, when considering the motivations of Muslim fundamentalist groups in Europe, such as those comprising Middle Eastern Palestinians and Kurds, North African Moroccans, and Asian Pakistanis residing in Britain, France, Germany, and Belgium, it is hard to determine whether their members are motivated by pure religious sentiments or whether they are mainly concerned with the political and cultural rights of their conationals in their homelands and host countries. This observation is particularly pertinent in view of the recent tendency to lump together all Muslim diasporic communities and to attribute solely ultra religious motivations and purposes to their violent actions.[11]

This difficult distinction is related to the debate about the role of religion in shaping the identity and behavioral patterns of ethnic entities in general and that of diasporic groups in particular. The argument here is that no totally homogeneous and coherent religious transnational entities act as fully unified collectives in launching violent and terrorist activities to pursue only Muslim ideas. Rather, most of the movements and organizations formed by diasporas like those mentioned previously—including some Al-Qaeda-linked groups—are closely connected to their respective ethnonational homelands and act in accordance with their perceived grievances.

The second distinction sets apart groups whose violent and terrorist activities are targeted at their homelands and those acting against their hostlands. Thus, Al-Qaeda, the Chechens and Pakistanis, for example, mainly target their host countries. The Basques, Palestinians, and Turkish Kurds, on the other hand, mostly support violent actions carried out by their brethren in their homelands and only occasionally support terrorism in their hostlands or other states. The differences between the terrorist activities these groups either initiate or support do not merely lie in their geographical locations but in the reasons, dynamics, and consequences that characterize their actions. These differences are discussed further later in the chapter.

Another distinction is between state-linked and stateless diasporas. Whereas the former maintains contacts and shares interests with the independent states in their homelands, such as the Jewish, Armenian, Iranian, and Pakistani diasporas, the latter group constitutes segments of nations who have not succeeded to establish a state of their own or whose homelands are dominated by other nation states, like the Palestinians, Kurds, and Tibetans. It seems clear that as a result of their full or partial integration into their host societies; their tendency to observe the law; and their inclination to protect and promote multiple cultural, political, and economic interests in their host countries, most diasporas in the first category are more reluctant to use violence and terrorism to promote their interests. These diasporas refrain to use terrorism also because of the restraint imposed on them by their homelands' governments. On the other hand, stateless diasporas are more prone to be engaged in violent and terrorist activities.

Causes and Motivations

The deeper causes and the more immediate motivations that lead ethnonational diasporic entities and their supporters to launch or to support violent and terrorist activities have not changed much throughout the last few decades. This is still the case in the aftermath of the collapse of the Soviet Union, which marked the end of the Cold War era, and during the recent period of globalization and glocalization.

One of the most prevalent causes and motivations for diasporic terrorism is a group's expulsion from its country of origin. Some, but not all, of the various Palestinian organizations serve as examples in this category. This includes, for instance, the Abu Nidal Organization, which is a stateless, transstate diasporic organization that carried out terrorist attacks in twenty countries killing or injuring almost 900 people and was supported by individuals and groups within the Palestinian diaspora in the West. Other Palestinian organizations established as a reaction to their expulsion from parts of Palestine in 1948 and then in 1967 are the Palestine Liberation Front and the Popular Front for the Liberation of Palestine. It is important to note that, because of Israeli control over the Palestinian-occupied territories, the headquarters of these and other Palestinian organizations are outside Palestine, such as in Syria.

Another common cause is the existence of struggles for separation and independence in one's homeland. One of the best-known organizations in this category is the ETA, which is supported by segments of the Basque diaspora. Palestinian organizations, such as Hamas, receive funding from Palestinian expatriates in the diaspora, from Iran, and from private benefactors in Saudi Arabia and in other Arab states. Some fund-raising and propaganda activities on behalf of Hamas take place in Western Europe and in both North and South America. Likewise, the PKK received a safe haven and modest aid from Syria, Iraq, and Iran, as well as financial and psychological support from the Kurdish diaspora. The LTTE, on the other hand, is closely connected to Tamil communities in North America, Europe, and Asia. Through these networks, some of which are involved in smuggling narcotics, the Tamil Tigers raise funds and supply their fighters in Sri Lanka.

A further motivation is the systematic discrimination of a group in its homeland. The Lebanese radical Shiite movement Hezbollah, for example, exists mainly to protect Shiite interests in Lebanon. However, because it also opposes Israel and is against peace negotiations with that state, it is regarded as a transnational diaspora. It has established cells in Europe, Africa, South America, North America, and Asia, and it receives substantial amounts of training; weapons; explosives; and financial, political, diplomatic, and organizational aid from Iran, Syria, and the Lebanese Shiite diaspora. Similar dynamics can be found in the case of the Islamic Movement of Uzbekistan; the Egyptian Islamic Jihad; the National Liberation Army of Iran; and the Revolutionary Armed Forces of Colombia.

Equally, discrimination in the diasporas' host countries can also become a cause or motivation for supporting terrorism. Examples include the Harakat ul-Mujahidin, an Islamic militant group based in Pakistan that operates primarily in Kashmir. Leaders of this organization have been linked to Osama bin Laden's Al-Qaeda and have signed his *fatwa* calling for attacks on U.S. and Western interests. It obtains donations from Saudi Arabia and other Islamic states, as well as from Pakistanis and Kashmiris in the diaspora. Another group in this category is the Jaish-e-Mohammad [Army of Mohammad], a Muslim group based in Pakistan that has also established connections to Al-Qaeda and to a number of Pakistani diasporic communities.

Legal and political persecution in the homeland is yet another related motivation for supporting terrorism. For example, Algerian expatriates, many of whom reside in Western Europe and especially in France, used to provide financial and logistic support to the GIA. The Egyptian Al-Gama'a al-Islamiyya has a diasporic external wing that displays a worldwide presence. The Revolutionary Organization 17 November is purported to have received assistance from groups in the Greek diaspora. Kach and Kahane Chai, two groups active in the struggle of ultra religious and nationalist Israeli Jews, were founded by a radical Israeli–American rabbi named Meir Kahane in the United States and are supported mainly by sympathizers in that country.

Other reasons for diasporic involvement with terrorism include blatant racism, religious and antireligious denigration, as well as connections to organized crime (see Atanas Gotchev's contribution in this book). Indeed, if we review the full list of these movements and organizations and examine quantitative data about the length and intensity of their campaigns as well as the volume of their violent and terrorist activities, it seems that except for Al-Qaeda and a few other culturally and religiously motivated organizations, the most active supporters of terrorism are ethnonational stateless diasporas. The second most relevant category appears to be those attempting to improve the cultural, political, and economic conditions in their homelands. These findings are further elaborated in the following section.

Dynamics

Since the 1990s, a clearer picture has emerged of the various diasporic entities' motivations, strategies, tactics, resources, means, and modes of operation. According to the expanding literature on diasporas, the most evident background factors that have not created but nevertheless have further motivated and facilitated the violent and terrorist activities of such entities are connected to the current trends of globalization, regionalization, glocalization, liberalization, and democratization. More specifically, the involvement of diasporas in subversive actions is facilitated by the increasing ease of transportation; the lack of control at most states' borders; the growing demand for foreign workers; the ramifications of pluralism, liberalization, democratization, and multiculturalism, mainly in democratic and democratizing host countries; and the widespread use of global means of communication.[12]

The most important characteristic of the diasporas' "hard cores," who use or support violence or terrorism, is the renewed substantial significance of the ethnonational identity, which in certain cases is enhanced by religious feelings. In all the cases presented earlier, including the Palestinians, Jews, Irish, and Tamils, identity is shaped and maintained as a result of the impact of strong primordial and mythical factors that are inseparably intertwined with the somewhat less important instrumental considerations.

Even if most of the existing ethnonational diasporas do not constitute tightly knit traditional communities and although they may be influenced by modern developments, their members' deeply rooted identities—and, more recently, their readiness to publicly identify as members of such entities—generate higher levels of cohesion and solidarity among the activist core members of these entities. In turn, the cohesion and solidarity of such entities are directly linked to their members' strong attachment to and contacts with their ethnonational homelands or to their venerated religious centers. In various cases, the religious beliefs, whether moderate or fundamentalist, held by individuals and core groups augment the mobilization of members, their dedication, and consequently their readiness either to carry out or to support insurgent actions. Whenever members of these core groups show strong commitment to follow their emotional and cognitive inclinations, they tend to develop ambiguous, dual, or divided loyalties to their host countries. As a consequence, some of them would be more inclined to perform terrorist acts or to support them.

Generally, stateless diasporas fighting for secession or independence in their homeland, such as the Palestinians, Irish, Turkish Kurds, and Kashmiris, have shown the greatest commitment and dedication to the support of insurgency in their homelands and on some occasions also in the hostlands. Likewise, such diasporas have been more active in aggressive publicity campaigns on behalf of their brethren in their homelands or in other host countries.

To make mobilization and insurgent activities effective, such groups must be highly organized and led by dedicated people. Both proletarians, such as the Kurds in Germany and the Algerians in France, and richer diasporas, such as the Jews and the Irish in the United States, have engaged in or have supported such insurgencies. However, though it is evident that the latter—who are better organized and have access to more economic, political, and other resources—can be more effective, they may at the same time be less committed to the cause of the entire dispersed nation. This has been the case with the Armenian and Greek diasporas when full independence of their homelands was achieved.

Resources

Except for diasporic mafias and criminal groups, and apart from the poorest and most deprived groups in both their host countries and homelands, pure economic interests or goals do not serve as the critical motivational factors or causes for terrorism. In fact, many of the activists and terrorists are educated and comparatively well off. Still, the mobilization of manpower, funds, and other resources are significant aspects of the phenomenon. In this respect, better educated and moderately wealthy diasporans have better chances to succeed.

Again, these are hardly new issues. Palestinians been engaged in these activities for decades, as have the Turkish Kurdish, Armenians, and, of course, the Jews. When the funding by homelands or by other states ceases, or when it becomes unobtainable or inaccessible, the importance of diasporic entities in mobilizing financial and other resources is considerably enhanced.[13] In the early 1990s, for example, the end of the Soviet Union's financial and military sponsorship caused the collapse of a number of insurgent and terrorist groups that had previously been dependent on Moscow. The same applies to all the groups that had received financial and other kinds of support from Saddam Hussein's Iraq. At the same time, the increase in the number of ethnic or communal insurgencies has heightened the relative significance of ethnonational diaspora support. For obvious reasons, accurate data on the volume of the various resources supplied to, and used by, terrorist groups are unavailable or extremely difficult to access. Neither the terrorist organizations and movements nor the relevant governments are ready to supply such data.[14]

Policy Implications

As the groups' reasons for using terrorism are firmly linked to their ideational and cultural aspirations as well as their ethnonational and religious beliefs and needs, the most essential and obvious policy suggestion is that all involved parties should try to solve the very basic conflicts and tensions among these groups. Genuine and systematic efforts directed at the resolution of such conflicts, including the most difficult task—the establishment of independent sovereign states for stateless nations and their diasporas—can meaningfully reduce the inclination to use terrorism. The case of the Irish is a good example of such a development.

It is clear that some of these conflicts, such as the Israeli–Palestinian or the Kurdish–Turkish confrontations, are impossible or extremely difficult to solve. Therefore, at the very least, honest attempts should be made at conflict management. For example, during various stages of the Israeli–Palestinian conflict this was successfully tried and led to a temporary reduction in terrorism. It is extremely important, for example, to reduce structural inequalities in homelands and host countries by eliminating minorities' discrimination, barriers to sociopolitical and socioeconomic mobility, deprivation, and the possession of full rights. Equally important is the need to mitigate the impact of rapid sociopolitical and socioeconomic changes. This should be done through long-term social, political, and economic aid and investments that would contribute to sustainable development and empower marginalized groups and individuals, especially women and young persons (see Ted Robert Gurr's contribution in this book).

It is important to try to ameliorate, even partially, the immediate social, political, and economic conditions that lead to terrorism by promoting political compromises and by providing opportunities for individual and collective disengagement from terrorism. Regional unions, nongovernmental organizations, the corporate sector, private financial institutions, and civil society generally should be encouraged to lead the formulation of strategies and should invest in plans aimed at reducing inequalities and discrimination affecting minorities and diasporas.

As we have seen, most existing diasporas are not tightly knit homogenous entities that collectively pursue a single strategy, especially not when it comes to terrorism. Nobody should postulate, therefore, that entire diasporic entities partake in terrorist activities or support them. In fact, in most cases—the Irish, Jewish, Turkish, Basque, or Kurdish diasporas spring to mind—only relatively small number of individuals and small groups of core members support such activities. In most cases, terrorism does not constitute a permanent strategy but rather a temporary tactic, which is intended to achieve social and political goals, and once these are achieved the diasporas' tactics change. It is also true that, historically, the use of terror as a tactic is confined to relatively short periods of crisis in the homelands, host countries, or in other states where their brethrens reside. Hence, the use of terror and violence does not transform entire communities into warrior communities.

Finally, it should be remembered that many of these groups are engaged in activities intended to enhance the cultural, civic, and economic well-being of their own communities, their host countries, and their homelands. Therefore, we should be careful not to stigmatize entire diasporic entities, thereby creating a permanently hostile environment that can make the lives of diasporans and diasporas even harder than they usually are and can push these people to use even more dangerous tactics and means.

Endnotes

1. Gerhard Mueller, "The Nature, Definition, and Uses of Terrorism, and the Range of Rational Options to Deal with It: A Summary," in *Meeting the Challenges of Global Terrorism. Prevention, Control and Recovery*, ed. Dunn Dilip and Peter C. Kratcoski (New York: Lexington Book, 2003); and "The War for Islam's Heart," *Economist*, September 18, 2004.

2. Walter Laqueur, "Postmodern Terrorism," *Foreign Affairs* 75, no. 5, pp 24-36, (1996).

3. Yehezkel Dror, *Crazy States: A Counter Conventional Strategic Problem* (Lexington, MA: Heath, 1974); see also Alex Schmid and Albert Jongman, *Political Terrorism: A New Guide to Actors, Authors, Concepts, Data Bases, Theories, and Literature* (New York: Transactions Publishers, 2005).

4. United Nations High Commissioner for Refugees, 56th General Assembly, Third Committee, November 19, 2001.

5. See Gabriel Sheffer, *Diaspora Politics: At Home Abroad* (Cambridge, UK: Cambridge University Press, 2003), ch. 4.
6. Victor Asal and Andrew Blum, "Holy Terror and Mass Killings? Mass Casualty Terrorism," *International Studies Review* 7, no. 1, pp. 153-155,, (2005).
7. For a list of these organizations, see for example, the Center of Defense Information at www.cdi.org.
8. U.S. State Department Counterterrorism Office, Patterns of Global Terrorism, Office of the Coordinator for Counterterrorism, 2005, www.state.gov.
9. Rand Corporation Policy Resources for Congress, Terrorism: Current and Long Term Threats. Testimony presented to the Senate Armed Services Committee on Emerging Threats, Nov. 15, 2001.
10. Sheffer, Diaspora Politics, chap. 3.
11. Rivka Yadlin, "The Muslim Diaspora in the West," in *Middle Eastern Minorities and Diasporas*, ed. Moshe Maoz and Sheffer, pp.219-230 (Brighton, UK: Sussex Academic Press, 2002); see also Riva Kastoryano, "The Reach of Transnationalism," in *Critical Views of September 11*, ed. Eric Hershberg and Kevin Moore, pp. 209-223 (New York: New Press, 2003).
12. See Michael Dahan and Sheffer, "Ethnic Groups and Distance Shrinking Communication Technologies," *Nationalism and Ethnic Politics* 7, no. 1, pp. 85-107, (2001).
13. See Aline Angoustures and Valerie Pascal, "Diasporas et Financement des Conflits," in *Economie des Guerres Civiles*, ed. Francois Jean Rufin and Jean-Christophe Rufin, pp. 495-542, (Paris: Hachette, 1996).
14. Lawrence Malkin and Yuval Elizur, "Terrorism's Money Trail," *World Policy Journal* 18, no. 1, pp. 60-70, (2001).

Culture and Religion

10

Religion as a Cause of Terrorism

Mark Juergensmeyer

The subway attacks in London in July 2005 brought back bitter memories of the Madrid train bombings in 2004, the World Trade Center assault in 2001, and the many suicide bombings in Iraq and Israel in recent years. In the wake of any terrorist attack the immediate questions are who and why: Who would do such a thing, and why would they want to do it? When religion is a part of the picture, the questions are compounded. This is the case whether the perpetrators are the Muslim activists in the London and Madrid bombings, jihadi resistance fighters in Iraq, Christian abortion clinic bombers in the United States, or violent Israeli settlers whom Prime Minister Ariel Sharon called Jewish terrorists during the dismantlement of settlements in Gaza and the West Bank in August 2005.

One of the enduring questions is what religion has to do with this—with them and what they did. Put simply, does religion cause terrorism? Could these violent acts be the fault of religion—the result of a dark strain of religious thinking that leads to absolutism and violence? Or has the innocence of religion been abused by wily political activists who twist religion's essential message of peace for their own devious purposes? Is religion the problem or the victim?

Each case in which religion has been linked to violence is different. So one could be justified in saying there is no one simple answer. Yet this has not stopped the media commentators, public officials, and academics whose generalizations about religion's role abound. Their positions may be found in the assumptions lurking behind policy choices and news media reports and within the causative theories about terrorism that the academics propose. Curiously, their positions are sometimes diametrically opposed. An example of the diversity of opinions may be found in two widely discussed books published in 2005: *Dying to Win: The Strategic Logic of Suicide Terrorism* by Robert A Pape and *Fighting Words: The Origins of Religious Violence* by Hector Avalos.[1]

The Argument That Religion Does Cause Terrorism

Avalos's book, *Fighting Words*, posits that religious terrorism is indeed caused by religion or, rather, that religion creates an imaginary supply of sacred resources over which humans contend. Avalos regards all forms of social and political conflict to be contests over scarce resources. The ones who do not have the scarce resources want them, and the ones that have them want to keep them. In the case of religious conflict the scarce resources are things that religion specifically supplies: the favor of God, blessings, and salvation. By definition these are not equally bestowed on everyone and must be earned and protected. When Rabbi Meir Kahane challenged Jews to restore God's honor, it was God's favor to the Jews that he wished to restore. Hence an ordinary battle is a conflict to earn the highest heavenly rewards.

From Avalos's point of view, moreover, the necessity of violence is often built into the very structure of religious commitment. The act of atonement in Christianity, the sense of revenge in Judaism, and the martial triumphalism of Islam all require violent acts to fulfill their religious images of the world. And in each case the result of violence is to bring the benefits of the scarce resources of spiritual blessings to the grateful perpetrator of the religious violence.

Avalos's position is controversial even in the academic community. Many observers have pointed out that current religious conflicts are seldom about religion per se—they are about national territory, political leadership, and socioeconomic control all cast in a religious light. Within the wider public there is perhaps even less support for the notion that religion in general leads directly to violent acts. Despite the rise of religious violence in recent years most people still regard religion—at least their own religion—as something benign. This attitude is prevalent even among members of religious communities from which violence has originated. Most Muslims regard Islam as a religion of peace, and Christians and Jews regard their own religion in the same way. Most of the faithful in these religions refuse to believe that their own beliefs could have led to violence.

Yet when one looks outside one's faith it is easier to blame religion. In the current climate of Muslim political violence, a significant sector of the American and European public assumes that Islam is part of the problem. Despite the cautionary words of President George W. Bush imploring Americans not to blame Islam for the September 11, 2001, attacks, a certain Islamophobia has crept into public conversation.

The implication of this point of view is the unfortunate notion that the whole of Islam has supported acts of terrorism. The inevitable attachment of Islam to terrorism in the ubiquitous phrase *Islamic terrorism* is one example of this habit of thinking. Another is vaunting the term *jihad* to a place of supreme Islamic importance, as if all Muslims agreed with its militarized usage by unauthorized extremist groups. The most strident expositions of this way of thinking are found in assertions of Christian televangelists such as Pat Robertson and Jerry Falwell that the Prophet himself was a kind of terrorist. More moderate forms are the attempts by political commentators and some scholars to explain—as if there was need for it—why Islam is so political. Even Connecticut's liberal senator Christopher Dodd, in a television interview in November 2003, cautioned Americans not to expect too much tolerance from Islam given its propensity for ideological control over public life. He referenced a book by historian Bernard Lewis for this point of view, which he recommended to the viewers.[2]

The assumption of those who hold the "Islam is the problem" position is that the Muslim relationship to politics is peculiar. But this is not true. Most traditional societies have had a close tie between political leadership and religious authority, and religion often plays a role in undergirding the moral authority of public life. In Judaism the Davidic line of kingship is anointed by God; in Hinduism the kings are thought to uphold divine order through the white umbrella of *dharma;* in Christianity the political history of Europe is rife with contesting and sometimes merging lines of authority between church and state. At the turn of the twenty-first century, violent Jewish, Hindu, and Christian activists have all, like their Muslim counterparts, looked to traditional religious patterns of politicized religion to justify their own militant stance.

The public life of contemporary America is no exception. It is one in which religion is very much involved with politics and politics with religion. The evangelical professions of faith of President Bush and advisers such as former attorney general John Ashcroft fuel the impression that U.S. foreign policy has a triumphant agenda of global Christendom. This characterization of religion's hand in U.S. politics is often exaggerated by foreign observers in Europe and the Middle East, but the Christian rhetoric of some members of the George W. Bush administration has been undeniable and lends credibility to such a view.

Even more troubling are strands of Christian theocracy that have emerged among extreme groups in the United States. Some employ violence in their opposition to secular society and their hatred of a globalized culture and economy. A neo-Calvinist theology of a religious state lies behind the bombing of abortion clinics and the shooting of abortion clinic staff by Lutheran and Presbyterian activists in Maryland and Florida. The Christian identity philosophy of race war and a government enshrining a white Christian supremacy lies behind Eric Robert Rudolph's attack on the Atlanta Olympic Park, other bombings of gay bars and abortion clinics, the killing of a Denver radio talk-show host, an assault on a Jewish day-care center in Los Angeles, and many other incidents—including Ruby Ridge—perpetrated by Christian militia in recent years. The so-called "Cosmotheism," based on Christianity, that was espoused by William Pierce and embraced by Timothy McVeigh was the ideological justification for McVeigh's bombing of the Oklahoma City Federal Building. In fact, there have been far more attacks by Christian terrorist groups on American soil in the last fifteen years than Muslim ones. Aside from September 11 and the 1993 attempt to destroy the World Trade Center, almost all of the other terrorist acts have been perpetrated by Christian theocracy.

Yet somehow, despite evidence to the contrary, the American public labels Islam as a terrorist religion rather than Christianity. The arguments that agree or disagree with this position often get mired in the tedious task of dredging up scriptural or historical examples to show the political and militant side of Islam—or contrarily, of other religions like Christianity, Judaism, or Hinduism. Then opponents challenge the utility of those examples, and the debate goes on. The arguments would not be necessary, however, if one did not assume that religion is responsible for acts of public violence in the first place.

The Argument That Religion Does Not Cause Terrorism

The position that religion is not the problem is taken by observers on the other side of the public discussion over religion after September 11. In some cases they see religion as an innocent victim; in other cases they see it as simply irrelevant. In *Dying to Win*, Robert Pape argued that religion is not the motive in most acts of suicide bombing. Looking at a broad swath of cases of suicide activists in recent years, Pape concluded that they are not motivated by a blind religious fervor as much as a calculated political attempt. The primary motive is to defend territory. Pape accurately pointed out that until 2003 the most suicide bombings were conducted not by a religious group but by a secular ethnic movement: the Tamil Tigers in Sri Lanka.

Pape based his conclusions on an analysis of the database maintained by the Chicago Project of Suicide Terrorism. He provided a demographic profile of over 460 men and women, though they are mostly men. They are not, he argued, "mainly poor, uneducated, immature religious zealots or social losers," as they have sometimes been portrayed.[3] What they have in common is the sense that their territory or culture has been invaded by an alien power that cannot easily be overthrown. In this desperate situation of social survival they turn to the simplest and most direct form of militant engagement: using their own bodies as bombs. Contrary to the perception of many, suicide bombers are not religious loners but are usually part of large militant organizations with well-honed strategies aimed at ousting foreign control from what they consider their own territory. The concessions made to such organizations in the past by the governments who have been opposed to them have given the organizations behind suicide bombings the confidence that their strategies work and are worth repeating.

Little is said about religion in Pape's book. Pape does devote a chapter describing how religion can intensify the main motivation of defending one's territory. But in general, in Pape's analysis, religious motives are beside the point. For this reason there is no attempt to explain the extraordinarily ubiquitous role of religion in violent movements around the world, from Sikh activists in India to Christian militia in Idaho to Muslim jihadis from Morocco to Bali. Nor is there any attempt to explain what difference religion makes when it enters into a conflict and religionizes the struggle, as both Muslim and Jewish extremists did in the Israel–Palestine dispute—a conflict that prior to the 1990s was largely a secular struggle over territorial control. One is left with the impression that, although Pape's study is useful in reminding us that acts of violence are about real things—such as the defense of culture and territory—it still does not explain why religion has become such a forceful and difficult vehicle for framing these concerns in recent years.

Nonetheless, appreciation for Pape's position has been widespread, in part because it appears to contradict the U.S. administration's position that Islamic militants are opposed to freedom. Pape argued that, to the contrary, freedom is precisely what they are fighting for. Moreover, his arguments buttress the position of two other, quite different camps: religious defenders eager to distance religion from the violent acts with which religion has recently been associated; and secular analysts who have always thought that secular factors, particularly economic and political concerns, are the main ingredients of social conflict.

This secular perspective is the one that lies behind the phrase commonly found in the news media and in the statements of political leaders, "the use of religion for political purposes." When this phrase is employed religion is dismissed of any culpability in creating an atmosphere of violence. A U.S. State Department official once told me that religion was being used throughout the Middle East, masking problems that were essentially economic in nature. He assured me that if jobs were to be had by unemployed Egyptians and Palestinians the problem of religious politics in these impoverished societies would quickly vanish. From his point of view it was unthinkable that religious activists would actually be motivated by religion, or at least by ideological views of the world that were framed in religious language. Similarly, Michael Sells's study of the role of Christian symbolism in resurgent Serbian nationalism, *The Bridge Betrayed*, was ridiculed by a reviewer for the *Economist* who saw the conflict as purely a matter of secular nationalism in which religion played no role.[4] The assumption of the reviewer, like that of the State Department official with whom I spoke, was that religion was the dependent variable, a rhetorical gloss over the real issues that were invariably economic or political.

From the perspectives of Pape and the State Department economist, religion is essentially irrelevant to the motivations of terrorism. Religious defenders agree and take this point of view a step further. They state that religion is not just neutral about violence; it is opposed to it, and thus it is an innocent victim of political activists. In some cases these religious defenders do not deny that there may be religious elements in the motives of violent activists, but they claim that these extreme religious groups do not represent the normative traditions. Most Buddhist leaders in Japan, for instance, distanced themselves from what they regarded as the pseudo-Buddhism of the Aum Shinrikyo sect implicated in the nerve gas attack on the Tokyo subways. Most Muslims refused to believe that fellow members of their faith could have been responsible for anything as atrocious as the September 11 attacks—and hence the popular conspiracy theory in the Muslim world that somehow Israeli secret police had plotted the terrible deed. Most Christians in America saw the religiosity of Timothy McVeigh as anti-Christian, even antireligious, and refused to describe him as a Christian terrorist, despite the strong Christian subtext of the novel *The Turner Diaries*, which McVeigh regarded as his Bible.[5]

Some scholars have come to the defense of religion in a similar way, by characterizing the religion of activists groups as deviant from the religious norm and therefore uncharacteristic of true religion. This is essentially the stance that Bruce Lawrence took in defending Islam in *Shattering the Myth*.[6] The term *fundamentalism*—applied not just to Christianity but to a whole host of religious traditions—is another way of excusing so-called normal religion and of isolating religion's problems to a deviant form of the species. It is used sometimes to suggest an almost viral spread of an odd and dangerous mutation of religion that if left on its own naturally leads to violence, autocracy, and other extremes. Fortunately, so this line of thinking goes, normal religion is exempt. Recently, however, *Islam* and *fundamentalism* are tied together so frequently in public conversation that the term *fundamentalism* has become a way of condemning all of Islam as a deviant branch of religion. But even in this case the use of the term *fundamentalism* allows for the defenders of other religions to take comfort in the notion that their kind of nonfundamentalist religion is exempt from violence or other extreme forms of public behavior.

These various points of view present us with two or perhaps three or four different answers to the question, Is religion a cause of terrorism? Avalos says yes, religion in general is a cause of terrorism. The Islamophobes say yes, Islam in particular is a problem. Pape says no, religion is irrelevant to the fight to defend territory. Other religious defenders say no, ordinary religion is innocent of violence, but some odd forms of religion might contribute to it.

The Argument That Religion Is Not the Problem but That It Is Problematic

It seems to me that it is not necessary to have to make one choice among these options. As anyone who has ever taken a multiple-choice test knows, there is a dilemma when presented with such absolute differences. The most accurate responses are often found in the gray categories: (c) none of the above; or (d) all of the above. In the case of the question regarding the involvement of religion in contemporary public life, the answer is not simply a matter of peculiar religion gone bad or of good religion being used by bad people. We know that there are strata of religious imagination that deal with all sides and moods of human existence—the peace and the perversity, the tranquility and the terror.

In my own studies of cases of religious violence, I have found that religious language and ideas play an important role, though not necessarily the initial one. The conditions of conflict that lead to tension are usually economic and social in character—and often, as Pape described them, a defense of territory or culture perceived to be under control by an outside power. At some point in the conflict, however, usually at a time of frustration and desperation, the political contest becomes religionized. Then what was primarily a secular struggle takes on the aura of sacred conflict. This creates a whole new set of problems.

Beginning in the 1980s, I have studied a variety of cases of contemporary religious activism. I started with the situation involving the Sikhs in the Punjab, a region in which I lived for some years and know fairly well. I have also observed the rise of Hindu political violence; the Muslim separatist movement in Kashmir; the Buddhist antigovernment protests in Sri Lanka; the Aum Shinrikyo movement in Japan; the Islamic revolution in Iran; Sunni jihadi movements in Egypt, Palestine, and elsewhere in the Middle East; militant Messianic Jewish movements in Israel; Catholic and Protestant militants in Northern Ireland; and the Christian militia in the United States.[7]

I found in all of these cases an interesting replication of a central thesis. Though each group was responding to its own set of local social, economic, and political factors, in all cases there was a common ideological component: the perception that the modern idea of secular nationalism was insufficient in moral, political, and social terms. In many cases the effects of globalization were in the background as global economic and communications systems undercut the distinctiveness of nation-state identities. In some cases the hatred of the global system was overt, as in the American Christian militia's hatred of the new world order and the Al-Qaeda network's targeting of the World Trade Center. Thus, the motivating *cause*—if such a term can be used—was the sense of a loss of identity and control in the modern world.

This sense of social malaise is not necessarily a religious problem, but it is one for which ideologies, both secular nationalist and religious transnational, provide ready responses. Hence, in each of the cases I examined, religion became the ideology of protest. Particular religious images and themes were marshaled to resist what were imagined to be the enemies of traditional culture and identities: the global secular systems and their secular nation-state supporters.

There were other similarities among these cases. In each case those who embraced radical antistate religious ideologies felt personally upset with what they regarded as the oppression of the secular state. They experienced this oppression as an assault on their pride and identity and felt humiliated as a result. The failures of the state—

though economic, political, and cultural—were often experienced in personal ways as humiliation and alienation, as a loss of selfhood.

It is understandable then, that the men—and they were usually men—who experienced this loss of pride and identity would lash out in violence the way that men often do when they are frustrated. Such expressions of power are meant to at least symbolically regain their sense of manhood. In each case, however, the activists challenged these feelings of violence through images of collective violence borrowed from their religious traditions: the idea of cosmic war.

The idea of cosmic war was a remarkably consistent feature of all of these cases. Those people whom we might think of as terrorists regarded themselves as soldiers in what they imagined to be sacred battles. I call such notions of warfare *cosmic* because they are larger than life. They evoke great battles of the legendary past, and they relate to metaphysical conflicts between good and evil. Notions of cosmic war are intimately personal but can also be translated to the social plane. Ultimately, though, they transcend human experience. Often activists employ images of sacred warfare that are found in every religious tradition—such as the battles in the Hebrew Bible (i.e., the Old Testament), the epics of Hinduism and Buddhism, and the Islamic idea of jihad. What makes religious violence particularly savage and relentless is that its perpetrators have placed such religious images of divine struggle—cosmic war—in the service of worldly political battles. For this reason, acts of religious terror serve not only as tactics in a political strategy but also as evocations of a much larger spiritual confrontation.

This brings us back to the question of whether religion is the problem. In looking at the variety of cases, from the Palestinian Hamas movement to Al-Qaeda and the Christian militia, it is clear to me that in most cases there were real grievances: economic and social tensions experienced by large numbers of people. These grievances were not religious. They were not aimed at religious differences or issues of doctrine and belief. They were issues of social identity and meaningful participation in public life that in other contexts were expressed through Marxist and nationalist ideologies. But in this present moment of late modernity, these secular concerns have been expressed through rebellious religious ideologies. The grievances—the sense of alienation, marginalization, and social frustration—are often articulated in religious terms and seen through religious images, and the protest against them is organized by religious leaders through the medium or religious institutions. Thus, religion is not the initial problem, but the fact that religion is the medium through which these issues are expressed is problematic.

What Religion Brings to a Violent Conflict

What is problematic about the religious expression of antimodernism, anti-Americanism, and antiglobalization is that it brings new aspects to conflicts that were otherwise not a part of them. For one thing, religion personalizes the conflict. It provides personal rewards—for example, religious merit, redemption or the promise of heavenly luxuries—to those who struggle in conflicts that otherwise have only social benefits. It also provides vehicles of social mobilization that embrace vast numbers of supporters who otherwise would not be mobilized around social or political issues. In many cases, it provides an organizational network of local churches, mosques, temples, and religious associations into which patterns of leadership and support may be tapped. It gives the legitimacy of moral justification for political encounter. Even more importantly, it provides justification for violence that challenges the state's monopoly on morally sanctioned killing. According to the familiar sociological dictum attributed to Max Weber, the state's authority is always rooted in the social approval of the state to enforce its power through the use of bloodshed—in police authority, punishment, and armed defense. Religion is the only other entity that can give moral sanction for violence and is therefore inherently at least potentially revolutionary.

Religion also provides the image of cosmic war, which adds further complications to a conflict that has become baptized with religious authority. The notion of cosmic war gives an all-encompassing world view to those who embrace it. Supporters of Christian militia movements, for instance, described their "aha" experience when they discovered the world view of the Christian identity totalizing ideology that helped them make sense of the modern world, of their increasingly peripheral role in it, and of the dramatic actions they can take to set the world right. It gives them roles as religious soldiers who can literally fight back against the forces of evil.

The image of cosmic war is a potent force. When the template of spiritual battle is implanted onto a worldly opposition it dramatically changes the perception of the conflict by those engaged in it and vastly alters the way that the struggle is waged. It absolutizes the conflict into extreme opposing positions and demonizes opponents by imagining them to be satanic powers. This absolutism makes compromise difficult to fathom and holds out the promise of total victory through divine intervention. A sacred war waged in a godly span of time need not be won immediately, however. The timeline of sacred struggle is vast, perhaps even eternal.

I once had the occasion to point out the futility—in secular military terms—of the Islamic struggle in Palestine to Abdul Aziz Rantisi, the late leader of the political wing of the Hamas movement. It seemed to me that Israel's military force was such that a Palestinian military effort could never succeed. Rantisi assured me that that "Palestine was occupied before, for 200 years." He explained that he and his Palestinian comrades "can wait again—at least that long."[8] In his calculation, the struggles of God can endure for eons. Ultimately, however, they knew they would succeed.

So religion can be a problematic aspect of contemporary social conflict even if it is not the problem, in the sense of the root causes of discontent. Much of the violence in contemporary life that is perceived as terrorism around the world is directly related to the absolutism of conflict. The demonization of enemies allows those who regard themselves as soldiers for God to kill with no moral impunity. Quite the opposite is true: They feel that their acts will give them spiritual rewards.

Curiously, the same kind of thinking has crept into some of the responses to terrorism. The war on terrorism launched by the U.S. government after September 11 is a case in point. To the degree that the war references are metaphorical and are meant to imply an all-out effort in the manner of previous administrations' war on drugs and war on poverty, it is an understandable and appropriate response. The September 11 attacks were, after all, hideous acts that deeply scarred the American consciousness, and one could certainly understand that a responsible government would want to wage an all-out effort to hunt down those culpable and to bring them to justice.

But among some who espouse a war on terrorism the militant language is more than metaphor. God's blessing is imagined to be bestowed on a view of confrontation that is, like cosmic war, all encompassing, absolutizing, and demonizing. What is problematic about this view is that it brings an impatience with moderate solutions that require the slow procedures of systems of justice. It demands instead the quick and violent responses of war that lend simplicity to the confrontation and a sense of divine certainty to its resolution. Alas, such a position can fuel the fires of retaliation, leading to more acts of terrorism instead of less.

The role of religion in this literal war on terrorism is in a curious way similar to religion's role in the cosmic war imagined by those perpetrating terrorism. In both cases religion is a problematic partner of political confrontation. Religion brings more to conflict than simply a repository of symbols and the aura of divine support. It problematizes a conflict through its abiding absolutism, its justification for violence, and its ultimate images of warfare that demonize opponents and cast the conflict in transhistorical terms.

Endnotes

1. See Hector Avalos, *Fighting Words: The Origins of Religious Violence* (New York: Prometheus Books, 2005); and Robert A. Pape, *Dying to Win: The Strategic Logic of Suicide Terrorism* (New York: Random House, 2005).
2. Bernard Lewis, *The Crisis of Islam: Holy War and Unholy Terror* (New York: Random House, 2003).
3. Pape, *Dying to Win*, 32.
4. Michael A. Sells, *The Bridge Betrayed: Religion and Genocide in Bosnia* (Berkeley: University of California Press, 1996).
5. Andrew Macdonald [William Pierce], *The Turner Diaries* (Hillsboro, WV: National Vanguard Books, 1978).
6. Bruce Lawrence, *Shattering the Myth: Islam Beyond Violence* (Princeton, NJ: Princeton University Press, 2000).
7. See Mark Juergensmeyer, *Terror in the Mind of God: The Global Rise of Religious Violence*, 3d ed. (Berkeley: University of California Press, 2003); and Juergensmeyer, *The New Cold War? Religious Nationalism Confronts the Secular State* (Berkeley: University of California Press, 1993).
8. Abdul Aziz Rantisi (cofounder and political leader of Hamas), interview with author, Khan Yunis, Gaza, March 1, 1998.

11

Terrorism and the Rise of Political Islam

John L. Esposito

As the U.S. attacks of September 11, 2001, and the war on global terrorism have tragically demonstrated, understanding the relationship of Islam to terrorism is critical to national and international security in the twenty-first century. Osama bin Laden and Al-Qaeda symbolize a global jihad, a network of extremist groups threatening Muslim countries and the West, whose roots have proved deeper and more pervasive internationally than most had anticipated. This new global threat, which emerged from the jihad against the Soviet Union's occupation of Afghanistan, has exploded across the Muslim world from Central, South, and Southeast Asia to Europe and America.

Since the late twentieth century, political Islam, often also referred to as Islamic fundamentalism and Islamism, has been a significant factor in the politics of predominantly Muslim countries as well as the primary language of political discourse and mobilization from North Africa to Southeast Asia. Islamic republics or governments were created in Sudan, Iran, General Zia ul-Haq's Pakistan, and the Taliban's Afghanistan. Muslim rulers have appealed to Islam to enhance their legitimacy, rule, and policies; mainstream movements and political parties have appealed to Islam for legitimacy and to mobilize popular support. Islamists have been elected president, prime minister, or deputy prime minister and to parliament and have served in cabinets in countries as diverse as Sudan, Egypt, Algeria, Jordan, Lebanon, Turkey, Kuwait, Bahrain, Yemen, Pakistan, Afghanistan, Malaysia, and Indonesia.

At the same time, extremist organizations have used violence and terrorism in the name of Islam to threaten and to destabilize governments and to attack government officials, institutions, and ordinary citizens in Muslim countries and the West. In discussing political Islam, however, it is important to distinguish between mainstream and extremist movements. The former participate within the political system, whereas the latter engage in terrorism in the name of Islam. Both have roots in a broader religious revival that has touched all major faiths in the past few decades, and both draw—to differing degrees depending on time and place—on interpretations of Islam. However, to understand them both and in particular to combat religious extremism and terrorism, it is important to recognize their relationship to one another and, more importantly, how they differ. These distinctions have serious implications on policy approaches. A strict military and security and law enforcement zero-tolerance approach to terrorism is necessary, though it will never be completely successful because open societies can always be infiltrated. Conversely, a zero-tolerance approach to mainstream movements will not only undermine civil society and the credibility of the West's commitment to democratization but will also produce the alienation and resentment that feeds the growth of terrorism.

Origins and Nature of Political Islam

Political Islam is in many ways the successor of failed nationalist ideologies and projects in the 1950s and 1960s, from the Arab nationalism and socialism of North Africa and the Middle East to the Muslim nationalism of post-independence Pakistan. Indeed, the founders of many modern Islamic movements were formerly participants in nationalist movements: the Egyptian Muslim Brotherhood's founder, Hasan al-Banna; Tunisia's Rashid Ghannoushi of the Renaissance Party; Algeria's Abbasi Madani of the Islamic Salvation Front; and Turkey's Ecmettin Erbakan, founder of the Welfare (Refah) Party.

The reassertion of Islam in politics is rooted in a contemporary religious revival or resurgence beginning in the late 1960s and 1970s that affected both personal and public life. On the one hand, many Muslims became more religiously observant, as demonstrated by their emphasis on prayer, fasting, dress, family values and by the revitalization of Islamic mysticism or Sufism. On the other hand, Islam reemerged as an alternative religiopolitical ideology to the perceived failures of more secular forms of nationalism, capitalism, and socialism. Islamic symbols, rhetoric, actors, and organizations became major sources of legitimacy and mobilization, informing political and social activism. Whereas governments and Islamic movements appealed to Islam, the authoritarian nature of many governments in the Arab and Muslim world made political organizing and meetings difficult, if not impossible. The mosque was the one institution the state had the most difficulty dominating or controlling. Religion, mosques, and mullahs became a rallying point when there was no space allowed for any other. The use of the mosque–mullah network was critical in the Iranian revolution as have been private (nongovernmental) mosques and their imams in Egypt and many other countries. The importance of clergy–mosque networks (Shii and Sunni) have been seen most recently in post-Saddam Hussein Iraq and among Shii throughout the Gulf. State-asserted authority over mosques and religious leaders has fed the radicalization of religio-political movements who saw the religious establishment co-opted, intertwined, and thus discredited as representative of true Islam.

More often than not, faith and politics have been intertwined causes or catalysts. And though they vary by country and region, there are common threads: a widespread feeling of failure and loss of self-esteem in many Muslim societies. Issues of political and social injustice, such as authoritarianism, repression, unemployment, inadequate housing and social services, maldistribution of wealth, and corruption, combined with concerns about the preservation of religious and cultural identity and values became prominent themes in Muslim discourse. Many blamed Western models of political and economic development for these failures. Once enthusiastically pursued as symbols of modernity, these models increasingly came under criticism as sources of moral decline and spiritual malaise. Consequently, many became disillusioned with the West and particularly with the United States. However, outside forces and petrodollars also served as catalysts for Islamic movements. Countries like Saudi Arabia, Iran, and Libya as well as wealthy individuals used their petrodollars to extend their influence internationally, to promote their religious–ideological worldviews and politics, and to support government Islamization programs as well as Islamist movements, both mainstream and extremist. By the late 1980s and 1990s international issues and actors increasingly played important roles in Muslim politics: the Soviet–Afghan War; sanctions against Hussein's Iraq; and the oppression and liberation of Muslims in Bosnia, Kashmir, and Chechnya.

Though the majority of Islamists have worked to bring about change through social and political activism within their societies, participating in electoral politics and civil society where permitted, a significant and dangerous minority of extremists—jihad groups from Egypt to Indonesia, Al-Qaeda, and other terrorists—believe they have a mandate from God. Their war is against rulers in the Muslim world and their societies whom they believe to be authoritarian, oppressive, corrupt, and un-Islamic, as well as the West. For extremists, Islam is not simply an ideological and political alternative but an imperative. Since it is God's command, implementation must be immediate, not gradual, and the obligation to implement is incumbent on all true Muslims. For these extremists, Muslims who remain apolitical or resist—individual Muslims or governments—are no longer regarded as Muslims but rather as atheists or unbelievers, or enemies of God, against whom all true Muslims must wage holy war, or jihad. Moreover, acts normally forbidden—such as stealing, murdering noncombatants, and terrorism—against Muslim and non-Muslim enemies alike are seen as required. They are religiously legitimated in what is portrayed as a cosmic war between good and evil, between the army of God and the forces of Satan. One man, Sayyid Qutb, stands out as the ideologue of militant Islam. Though executed in 1966, his worldview has both directly and indirectly influenced extremist groups and movements for half a century.

Sayyid Qutb: Ideologue and Martyr of Islamic Radicalism

It would be difficult to overestimate the role played by Egypt's Sayyid Qutb (1906–66) in the rise of political Islam and in particular in the ideology of militant jihad. He has been both a respected intellectual and religious writer whose works include an influential commentary on the Quran and the ideologue for Muslim extremist movements around the globe. His journey from educated intellectual, government official, and admirer of the West to militant ideologue and activist who condemned both the Egyptian and American governments and defended the legitimacy of militant jihad influenced and inspired many militants from the assassins of Anwar Sadat to the followers of Osama bin Laden and Al-Qaeda.

Qutb had a modern education and became an official in the Ministry of Public Instruction as well as a poet and literary critic. Qutb's visit to America in the late 1940s proved to be a turning point in his life, transforming him from an admirer into a severe critic of the West. His experiences in America provided a culture shock that made him more religious and convinced him of the moral decadence of the West. Shortly after he returned to Egypt, Qutb joined the Muslim Brotherhood. He quickly emerged as a major voice in the Brotherhood and its most influential ideologue amid the growing confrontation with the Egyptian regime. Imprisoned and tortured for alleged involvement in a failed attempt to assassinate Gamal Abd al-Nasser, he became increasingly militant and radicalized, convinced that the Egyptian government was un-Islamic and must be overthrown.

Qutb's revolutionary vision is set forth in his most influential tract, Milestones.[1] His ideas have reverberated in the radical rhetoric of revolutionaries from Ayatollah Khomeini to bin Laden.

Qutb sharply divided Muslim societies into two diametrically opposed camps: the forces of good and of evil, those committed to the rule of God and those opposed, the party of God and the party of Satan. There was no middle ground. He emphasized the need to develop a special group—a vanguard—of true Muslims within this corrupt and faithless society. Since the creation of an Islamic government was a divine commandment, he argued, it was not an alternative to be worked toward. Rather, it was an imperative Muslims must strive to implement or must impose immediately. Indeed, given the authoritarian and repressive nature of the Egyptian government and many other governments in the Muslim world, Qutb concluded that jihad as armed struggle was the only way to implement the new Islamic order. For Qutb, jihad, as armed struggle in the defense of Islam against the injustice and oppression of anti-Islamic governments and the neocolonialism of the West and the East (i.e., Soviet Union), was incumbent on all Muslims. Those who refused to participate were to be counted among the enemies of God and should be excommunicated or declared unbelievers, or *takfir,* and fought and killed along with the other enemies of God. Qutb's radicalized world view became a source for ideologues from the founders of Egypt's Islamic Jihad to bin Laden and Al-Qaeda's call for a global jihad.

The Globalization and Hijacking of *Jihad*

In the late twentieth and early twenty-first centuries, because of Muslim politics and global communications, *jihad* has become even more widespread and complex in usage.[2] The importance of jihad is rooted in the Quran's command to struggle—the literal meaning of the word *jihad*—in the path of God and in the example of the Prophet Muhammad and his early Companions. In its most general meaning, jihad refers to the obligation incumbent on all Muslims, individuals, and the community to follow and realize God's will: to lead a virtuous life and to spread Islam through preaching, education, example, and writing. Jihad also includes the right, indeed the obligation, to defend Islam and the Muslim community from aggression.

These two broad meanings of jihad—as spiritual–moral and as armed struggle—are contrasted in a prophetic tradition in which Muhammad is reported to have said, "We return from the lesser jihad [warfare] to the greater jihad [the personal struggle to live a moral life]." Historically jihad has been subject to many interpretations and usages: spiritual and political, peaceful and violent, legitimate and illegitimate. Jihad has been interpreted and misinterpreted to justify resistance and liberation struggles, extremism and terrorism, and holy and unholy wars. In addition to historic battles and wars to protect Muslim peoples and lands, rulers from early caliphs to heads of modern states like Hussein have used jihad to legitimate campaigns that could spread the boundaries of their states or empires. Extremists past and present—from the Kharajites who assassinated the fourth caliph Ali to the assassins of Egypt's President Anwar Sadat, bin Laden, and Al-Qaeda, and a host of extremist movements from Morocco to Indonesia—have justified their acts of violence and terror by calling them acts of jihad.

In recent decades, jihad's primary Quranic religious or spiritual meanings, the struggle or effort to follow God's path and to build a just society, became more multifaceted and contemporary in its applications—for example, leading to a jihad to create a more just society or to engage in educational, community, and social service projects. At the same time, in response to authoritarian regimes and political conflicts, jihad became a clarion call used by resistance, liberation, and terrorist movements alike to legitimate their cause, to mobilize support, and to motivate their followers. The Afghan Mujahiddin, the Taliban, and the Northern Alliance each waged a jihad in Afghanistan against foreign powers and among themselves; Muslims movements in Kashmir, Chechnya, Daghestan, and the southern Philippines, Bosnia, and Kosovo have fashioned their struggles as jihads; Hizbollah, Hamas, and Islamic Jihad Palestine characterized war with Israel as a jihad; Algeria's Armed Islamic Group engaged in a jihad of terror against the government and their fellow citizens; and bin Laden and Al-Qaeda waged a global jihad against Muslim governments and the West. The terms *jihad* and *martyrdom*, or *shahid*, gained such currency and proved to be such powerful symbols that they were also used by nationalist, or secular, leaders and movements such as Yasser Arafat and the secular Palestinian National Authority and its military wing the al-Aqsa Martyrs Brigades.

The Soviet–Afghan war marked a new turning point as a jihad armed struggle went global to a degree never seen in the past. The *mujahidin* holy war drew Muslims from many parts of the world and support from Muslim and non-Muslim countries and sources. Those who fought in Afghanistan, called Afghan Arabs, moved on to fight other jihads in their home countries and in Bosnia, Kosovo, and Central Asia. Others stayed on or were trained and recruited in the new jihadi madrasas [religious schools] and training camps, joining in bin Laden's global jihad against Muslim governments and the West.

Although the distinction is often made between Quranic pre-scriptions about just war versus unjust war, many and conflicting interpretations of the verses have been made over time. At issue are the meaning of terms like *aggression* and *defense* and questions about when the command to sacrifice life and property to defend Islam is appropriate and how to define the enemies of Islam. For exam-ple, the Quran speaks repeatedly of the "enemies of God" and the "enemies of Islam," often defining them as "unbelievers." Although other Quranic verses appear to make it clear that such people should be physically fought against only if they behave aggressively toward Muslims, some Muslims have interpreted the call to struggle or strive against such enemies to be a permanent engagement required of all Muslims of every time and place until the entire world is converted to Islam. A major example of this kind of thinking would be those responsible for the attacks on the World Trade Center and the Penta-gon in the United States on September 11, 2001.

Terrorists like bin Laden and others have gone beyond classical Islam's criteria for a just jihad and recognize no limits but their own, employing any weapons or means. Adopting Qutb's militant world view of an Islam under siege, they ignore or reject Islamic law's regu-lations regarding the goals and means of a valid jihad: that violence must be proportional; that only the necessary amount of force should be used to repel the enemy; that innocent civilians should not be tar-geted; and that jihad must be declared by the ruler or head of state. Moreover, extremists have departed from the traditional Muslim view of armed jihad as a collective community responsibility and have asserted that jihad is an individual duty required of every Muslim.

Suicide Bombing and Terrorism

The most controversial and increasingly widespread form of jihad has been suicide bombing. The use of suicide terrorism has become a weapon of choice. It was used in the September 11 attacks against the World Trade Center and the Pentagon, and subsequently in extremist attacks globally, in particular in its widespread use in post-Hussein Iraq. Historically, Sunni and Shii Muslims have forbidden religious suicide and acts of terrorism. The Nizari Ismailis, popularly called the Assassins, who in the eleventh and twelfth centuries were notori-ous for sending suicidal assassins against their enemies, were rejected by mainstream Islam as fanatics. However, in the late twentieth cen-tury, the issue resurfaced as many, Shii and Sunni alike, engaged in suicide bombings, legitimating their actions religiously with terms like *jihad* and *martyrdom*. Although the origins of suicide attacks are often equated with Hamas in the Israeli–Palestinian conflict, in fact suicide bombings in the Muslim world first occurred in Lebanon, used by Hizbollah and al-Jihad in attacks such as those against the U.S. Marine barracks and French military headquarters in Beirut in 1983 in which 241 American troops were killed.

Suicide bombing later became the weapon of last resort in the Israel–Palestine conflict, often associated with Hamas, a religious, social, political, and military movement that emerged in late 1987 and was the product of Israeli occupation of the West Bank and Gaza. The combination of political and social activism with guerrilla warfare won financial and moral support from many Palestinians and sympathetic supporters in the broader Arab and Muslim world.[3] However, the actions of the Qassim Brigade, the Hamas military wing, earned Hamas its reputation for terrorism. Created in 1991, the brigade initially engaged in well-planned selective attacks against Israeli military and police. Organized into small clandestine cells, it used guerrilla warfare, not random acts of violence, to respond to Israeli policies and actions.

This position changed dramatically after the Oslo Accords in 1993. Responding to specific events in Israel and the West Bank and Gaza, in what they claimed was an escalation of Israeli repression of targeted assassinations, mass detentions, and deportations, the Qassim Brigade undertook direct attacks outside the heart of Israel against civilian as well as military targets. It adopted a new type of warfare: suicide bombing. Its deadly attacks increased exponentially after a Jewish settler killed twenty-nine worshippers during the Friday congregational prayer at the Mosque of the Patriarch in Hebron on February 25, 1994. The brigade promised swift revenge and retaliation for the massacre and undertook five anti-Israeli operations within Israel itself in cities like Galilee, Jerusalem, and Tel Aviv. The use of suicide bombing by Hamas further increased during the Second Intifada, which began in 2000, and also became more indiscriminate. Suicide bombing was justified by Hamas as a weapon of last resort in response to the Israeli military's overwhelming military superiority. They believed that suicide bombers were committing not an act of suicide but one of self-sacrifice, engaged in political resistance and retaliation against Israeli occupation and oppression.

Hamas provides an excellent example of diverse strategic responses to a complex and changing political context. It has had a strong political wing that has engaged in political opposition to Israel and the Palestinian Liberation Organization (PLO) and has participated in university student elections and, more recently, municipal elections. At the same time, it spawned a militia that initially engaged the Israeli military with conventional weapons. Hamas turned to suicide bombing in response to what it perceived as a changing context in which suicide bombers were its most effective weapon, especially in striking terror in the hearts of Israel's citizens with the hope that this would pressure the Israeli government to withdraw its military as it had done in Lebanon in May 2000. The attitude of Hamas toward the use of violence is a reminder of the pattern of many groups and movements. Whereas mainstream Islamic activists operate within the system, extremists believe that the nature of the particular political context is such that violent opposition is required—indeed, divinely mandated. At the same time, Hamas demonstrated in 2005-2006, the extent to which some movements adapt their strategies and policies in light of experiences and changing political contexts. While refusing to surrender its arms, Hamas did decide to participate as a political party in the January 2006 Palestinian parliamentary elections. In a stunning victory, Hamas swept the elections, winning a majority of the parliamentary seats and the right to form a government.

Hizbollah, which initiated the use of suicide bombing in the Middle East in 1983, provides another important and influential example of the tendency of movements to define and to adjust their strategy in response to political contexts. Hizbollah began as an Iranian-supported militia movement in Lebanon in response to the Israeli invasion of Lebanon. It used guerilla warfare and in 1983 turned to suicide bombing to drive the American and French military forces out of Lebanon. When the political context changed after the Taif Accords in 1989, Hizbollah became a major player in electoral politics as a political party and significant presence in the Lebanese parliament. However, it refused to lay down its arms in the south of Lebanon where it continued to fight what it regarded as an Israeli occupation. Indeed, the Israeli pullout in 2000—after twenty-two years of occupation—was widely seen by many, in particular militant Islamists, as vindicating the tactical use of violence and suicide bombing.

Suicide bombing has precipitated a sharp debate in the Muslim world, garnering both support and condemnation on religious grounds, with prominent religious leaders differing sharply in their legal opinions (*fatwa*). Sheikh Ahmad Yasin, the late religious leader and founder of Hamas, and Akram Sabri, the mufti, or legal expert, of Jerusalem, as well as many other Arab and Palestinian religious leaders argued that suicide bombing is necessary and justified. Other religious leaders and scholars condemned suicide bombings—in particular those that target civilians—as terrorism. Sheikh Abdulaziz bin Abdallah Al-Sheikh, Grand Mufti of Saudi Arabia, condemned all suicide bombing as suicide and therefore un-Islamic and forbidden by Islam. However, Sheikh Muhammad Sayyid Tantawi, the former grand mufti of Egypt and current rector of Al-Azhar University, drew a sharp distinction between suicide bombings that are acts of self-sacrifice and self-defense and the killing of noncombatants, women, and children, which he has consistently condemned. Sheikh Yusuf al-Qardawi, among the most influential religious authorities in the world, has given *fatwas* that recognize suicide bombing in Israel–Palestine as an act of self-defense, the giving of one's life for God with the hope that God will grant Paradise. Qardawi has legitimated the killing of civilians, arguing that Israel is a militant and military society in which both men and women serve in the military and reserves and that if an elderly person or a child is killed in such acts, it is an involuntary killing. At the same time, he has denounced acts of terrorism elsewhere as un-Islamic or against the teachings of Islam.

Osama bin Laden and the Spread of Global Terrorism

The suicide attacks of September 11, 2001, were a watershed in the history of political Islam and global terrorism, signaling the magnitude of the threat of bin Laden and Al-Qaeda and the globalization of jihad.[4] Bin Laden, the educated, wealthy son of a prominent Saudi family with close ties to the House of Saud, had fought against the Soviets in Afghanistan. The struggle allied him with a cause supported by the United States, Saudi Arabia, Pakistan, and many others. However, after the war he became radicalized by the prospect of an American-led coalition in the 1991 Gulf War and the subsequent increased presence and influence of America in Saudi Arabia and the Gulf. His opposition to the war escalated rapidly, resulting in his loss of Saudi citizenship, his move to Sudan, and then his return to Afghanistan, which became the primary training base for Al-Qaeda and its global jihad against Muslim governments as well as America and the West.

Bin Laden became the godfather of an emerging global terrorism, a major funder of terrorist groups, and a suspect in the 1993 bombing of the World Trade Center, of the slaughter of eighteen American soldiers in Somalia, and of bombings in Riyadh in 1995 and in Dhahran in 1996. He threatened attacks against Americans who remained on Saudi soil and promised retaliation internationally for cruise missile attacks against Sudan and his reported base in Afghanistan.[5] In February 1998, bin Laden and other militant leaders announced the creation of The Islamic Front for Jihad against Jews and Crusaders, a transnational coalition of extremist groups. Al-Qaeda was linked to a series of acts of terrorism: the truck bombing of American embassies in Kenya and Tanzania on August 7, 1998, that killed 263 people and injured more than 5,000, followed on October 12, 2000, by a suicide bombing attack against the *USS Cole*, which killed seventeen American sailors.

Osama bin Laden's message was primarily political rather than theological; he appealed to the grievances and popular causes of many in the Arab and Muslim world. A sharp critic of American foreign policy, he denounced the substantial American military and economic involvement and presence in Saudi Arabia and the Gulf, which he dismissed as Zionist crusaders; U.S. support for Israel; sanctions against Saddam's Iraq that resulted in the deaths of hundreds of thousands of civilians; Saudi Arabia; and other un-Islamic governments. To these were added other populist causes like Bosnia, Kosovo, Chechnya, and Kashmir. Bin Laden's intentions were forcefully stated in "A Declaration of War against the Americans" in 1996. Bin Laden declared he was fighting U.S. foreign policy in the Middle East and, in particular, American support for the House of Saud and the state of Israel. His goal, he said, was to unleash a clash of civilizations between Islam and the Zionist crusaders of the West to provoke an American backlash that would radicalize the Muslim world and would topple pro-Western Muslim governments.

Bin Laden and Al-Qaeda represented a new international brand of Sunni militancy and terrorism associated with the Afghan Arabs—those who had come from the Arab and Muslim world to fight alongside the Afghan *mujahideen* against the Soviets. The sources and growth of extremism and acts of terrorism were not confined to the Middle East but also encompassed Central, South, and Southeast Asia and later spread to America and Europe. Bin Laden and his chief of staff, Ayman al Zawahiri, were committed to a global jihad.

*****

There can be no doubt that religion provides a powerful source of authority, meaning, and legitimacy. Religiously motivated or legitimated violence and terror adds the dimensions of divine or absolute authority buttressing the authority of terrorist leaders, religious symbolism, moral justification, motivation and obligation, certitude, and heavenly reward that enhance recruitment and a willingness to fight and die in a sacred struggle (see Mark Juergensmeyer's contribution in this book). Thus, even more secular movements have appealed to and have used religion. The power of religious symbolism could be seen, for example, when Arafat, leader of the secular nationalist movements PLO and then PNA, used the terms *jihad* and *shahid* to describe his situation when he was under siege in Ramallah. The Palestinian militia—not just the Islamist Hamas—appropriated religious symbolism, choosing to call itself the Al-Aqsa Martyrs Brigade and drawing on the symbols of jihad and martyrdom. Moreover, though religious and nonreligious organizations and movements, whether Al-Qaeda or the Marxist Tamil Tigers, share a common strategy, Muslims often identify their goal as Islamic: to create an Islamic government, a caliphate, or simply a more Islamically oriented state and society.

However, Muslim political terrorism can boomerang and alienate segments of a society that might otherwise be sympathetic. A major turning point in the Egyptian government's war against extremists like Al-Jihad and the Gamaa Islamiyya occurred when the attacks in Luxor and elsewhere indiscriminately slaughtered innocent foreigners and civilian Egyptians. Similarly, despite the fact that the vast majority of those responsible for attacks against the World Trade Center and the Pentagon were Saudis, both the Saudi government and the populace became concerned and aggressive in combating Al-Qaeda and terrorism only after major attacks in Saudi Arabia targeted and killed Saudis, including women and children.

A critical issue in the war against global terrorism is the issue of legitimate versus illegitimate uses of violence. The problem is compounded by religious authority. Islam lacks a central authority: a single religious authority, hierarchy, or board of senior clergy. This can be a source of healthy diversity and flexibility. For example, based on jurist interpretations of texts and social contexts, muftis can render differing opinions, or *fatwas,* in such cases as contracts, marriage, divorce, and maintenance. This lack of a central authority, however, has also led to a war of *fatwas.* The problem can be seen in the diverse and conflicting rulings regarding suicide bombing in general and its use in the Israeli–Palestinian conflict; the sharp differences between mainstream religious leaders like Ayatollah Sistani and the actions of militants like Moqtedar al-Sadr or Abu Musab al-Zarqawi; the rulings of the mufti of Saudi Arabia; and the actions of al-Qaeda in Saudi Arabia.

The war against global terrorism will continue to challenge European and American policymakers as well as Muslim governments not only to use military and economic means but also to emphasize public diplomacy. The military can kill, capture, and contain terrorists, but, as we have seen, this has not lessened the growth of Muslim extremism and terrorism. Terrorists must be marginalized and delegitmated. Attempts to win the hearts and minds and to wage an ideological counteroffensive in this war of ideas require substantive foreign policy reforms. The primary causes or motivations of terrorism—the political and economic conditions and grievances that feed anger, alienation, and rage—must be addressed and ameliorated.

Drawing a sharp distinction between mainstream and extremist movements remains critical. Whereas terrorists require a security policy with zero tolerance, mainstream Islamists, especially political parties, require engagement by their governments and Western governments. If they are not allowed to vote or be in positions of political power but are banned or repressed, the risk of alienation and radicalization is significant. As we have seen, terrorists can be killed and captured but not completely eliminated. Post-September 11, many major terrorist leaders remain at liberty, and the numbers of terrorists and groups continue to grow. The greater challenge is to limit the growth of global terrorism, to address critical political and ideological factors, and thus to drain the fuel that ignites and the theologies of hate that reinforce and legitimate global terrorism.

Muslim religious leaders and intellectuals play a critical role in the ideological war against Muslim extremism and terrorism, which is the struggle for the soul of Islam. They bring to bear a religious authority and interpretations of Islam that discredit theologies of hate. They formulate and seek to implement doctrinal and educational reforms—in schools, madrasas, and universities—that more effectively respond to the challenges of globalization in the twenty-first century with its need for all religious faiths to emphasize inclusive rather than exclusive theologies that foster mutual understanding, religious pluralism, and tolerance. Finally, it is important to remember that Muslim societies have long been the most frequent victims of religious extremism and terrorism. The vast majority of Muslims and the majority of Islamic movements and activists desire and are one of the most important forces for securing stable and safe societies, representative governments, and the rule of law.

Endnotes

1. Milestones (Cedar Rapids, Iowa: United Publications, nd). See also John L. Esposito, *Unholy War: Terror in the Name of Islam*, ch. 2 (New York: Oxford University Press, 2003), and Ahmad Moussalli, *Radical Islamic Fundamentalism: The Ideological and Political Discourse of Sayyid Qutb* (Syracuse: Syracuse University Press, 1993).

2. For this discussion, I drew from John L. Esposito, *Unholy War: Terror in the Name of Islam* (New York: Oxford University Press, 2003); and Esposito, *The Islamic Threat: Myth or Reality?* 3rd ed. (New York: Oxford University Press, 1999).

3. Among the better studies of Hamas as well as its use of suicide are Shaul Mishal and Avraham, Sela Palestinian Hamas (New York: Columbia University Press 2000); Khaled Hroub, *Hamas: Political Thought and Practice* (Washington, D.C.: Institute for Palestine Studies, 2000); Robert Pape, *Dying to Win: The Strategic Logic*

of Suicide Bombing (New York: Random House, 2005); and Jean-Francois Legrain, "Hamas: Legitimate Heir of Palestinian Nationalism?" in *Political Islam: Revolution, Radicalism, or Reform?* ed. John L. Esposito (Boulder, CO: Lynne Rienner, 1997).

4. For perceptive discussions of Osama bin Laden, see Peter L. Bergen, *The Osama bin Laden I Know* (New York: Free Press, 2006); *Holy War Inc.* (New York: Free Press, 2002); Jason Burke, *Al-Qaeda: The True Story of Radical Islam* (London: I.B. Tauris, 2004); Ahmed Rashid, *Taliban: Militant Islam* (New Haven, CT: Yale University Press, 2001); and J. K. Cooley, *Unholy Wars: Afghanistan, America and International Terrorism* (London: Pluto Press, 2000).

5. Transcript of Osama bin Laden Interview, CNN/Time, August 25, 1998.

12

Terrorism and Deculturation

Olivier Roy

A popular view among journalists and experts is that of Islamic terror-ism as an expression of the Muslim wrath. According to this notion, a minority vanguard—the terrorists—uses unacceptable means to express a whole community's grievances. It is a reaction of a community that feels under threat: a response to Western encroachments in the Middle East and the imposition of Western values on Muslims living in the West. In reality, although it is obvious that many Muslims do react negatively to what they see as both a political and a cultural aggression, a closer analysis of the Islamic terrorists who struck the West in 2001 and continue to commit terrorist activity in presently seems to largely debunk the idea that their struggle has something to do with a clash of culture or civilizations or religions—even if they sometimes use such terms.

Where Do They Come From?

If we analyze the violent Islamic militants who have operated in West-ern Europe since the early 1990s, a clear pattern emerges. These indi-viduals, even when they have a Middle Eastern familial background, do not come from the Middle East to perpetrate terrorist attacks in the West, nor are they sent by a Middle Eastern terrorist organization with a local agenda, such as the liberation of Palestine.[1] They are part of the deterritorialized, supranational Islamic networks that operate in the West and at the periphery of the Middle East. Their backgrounds have little to do with Middle Eastern conflicts or traditional religious education, except the few Saudis and Yemenis who carried out the September 11, 2001, attacks on the United States. On the contrary, they are based in Europe, fluent in Western languages, and Western educated: None of them underwent a religious curriculum in Islamic madrassas, or religious schools. Some were born in Europe; others came as children, students, or political refugees; many even possessed Western citizenship. All of the September 11 pilots and their accomplices, except the Saudis' muscle, left their countries of origin to study abroad, especially scientific or technical subjects. They all have secular backgrounds with Western habits like drinking and dating girls until the days of their return, or conversion, to Islam. All broke with or dissociated themselves from their families. Though they were settling in the West, they were never involved in the local Muslim community life or with any religious congregation. Almost none of them made endogamic marriages with cousins or those from the same villages. In fact, many married non-Muslim Europeans, who, in many cases, converted to Islam.

In other words, they were cultural outcasts, living at the margin of society in either their countries of origin or their host countries. More interestingly, all of them—following normal lives in their countries of origin or in Western Europe—became born-again Muslims in Europe. The mosques of Hamburg, al-Qods, London, Finsbury Park, Marseilles, and even Montreal played a bigger role than a Saudi madrassa in the process of their radical Islamization. More recently, in 2004 to the present, the radicalization is happening outside the mosque, such as within a group of local friends, or indeed in jail. In any case, the main point is that they are Westernized and deterritorialized, meaning that they are not linked with a given country, including their family's country of origin. Their groups are often mixes of educated middle-class leaders and working-class dropouts, a pattern common to most of the West European radicals of the 1970s and 1980s; these groups include the German Red Army Faction, the Red Brigades in Italy, and Action Directe in France.

In almost every Al-Qaeda cell in Europe, we now find converts. They share many common patterns with the born-again Muslims. A few are middle class—usually the leaders, like Christian Caze in France who was a medical doctor killed in action against the police in Roubaix in 1996—whereas many are dropouts from working class, such as the American "dirty bomber" José Padilla, "shoe bomber" Richard Reid, London subway attacker Germaine Lindsay, and Frenchman Lionel Dumont who fought in Bosnia. Twenty years ago, such individuals would have joined radical leftist movements, but these have disappeared from the spaces of social exclusion or have become bourgeois like the Revolutionary Communist League in France, which took 5 percent in the last presidential election. Now only two movements of radical protest in the West claim to be internationalist: the antiglobalization movement and radical Islamists. To convert to European Islam is a way for a rebel to find a cause. It follows that the second generation of Al-Qaeda militants, who were recruited after 1992, is characterized precisely by the breaking of their ties with the allegedly "real" Muslim world they pretend to represent. Clearly, they are all far more a product of a Westernized Islam than of traditional Middle Eastern politics. However "old time" their theology may sound to Westerners, and whatever they may think of themselves, they are clearly more a postmodern phenomenon than a premodern one.

Thus, far from representing a traditional religious community or culture, these militants broke with their own past, and with traditional Islam, and experienced an individual re-Islamization in a small cell of uprooted fellows, where they forged their own Islam. This is illustrated vividly, for example, by Mohammed Atta, who stated that he did not want to get buried according to Egyptian tradition, which he dubbed un-Islamic. These militants do not follow any school or notable cleric in Islam and often live according to non-Muslim standards. Indeed, though *taqiya*, or hiding one's ideas, is a popular explanation for such behavior, it is hard to see how drinking and trying to hire prostitutes the night before a terrorist act—as did some of the September 11 terrorists—would be a good way to deceive the enemy. After all, secret agents are supposed to know how not to attract attention. Moreover, *taqiya* is a Shi'a notion and is considered an innovation in the Sunni world.

Whom Do They Fight?

Terrorists' conception of space has little to do with the defense of Darul Islam, the traditional territory where Muslims live under Muslim rulers. First, they usually do not consider that the present rulers are legitimate, yet they do not fight to replace them by true Islamic leaders. Al-Qaeda—from Afghanistan, Bosnia, and Chechnya to New York and Fallujah—is fighting first of all against the West or its supposed allies (e.g., Jews and Shi'as) but not against the present regimes. Al-Qaeda has been involved in attacks against Jewish targets but almost never against Israeli targets. And even in Saudi Arabia, they are targeting foreigners rather than local government officials. In fact, this is precisely because they see Darul Islam as a deterritorialized concept: wherever Muslims are under pressure is a good place to fight.

Al-Qaeda's fight started long before any Western military encroachment in the Middle East or Afghanistan. The predecessor of Osama bin Laden—Abdullah Azzam, a Palestinian Muslim brother—gave up the fight to free Palestine, because in his view this was a nationalist struggle rather than a purely religious jihad. No European Al-Qaeda member left Europe or the United States to fight for Islam in his or his family's country of origin, except some Pakistanis. They preferred Bosnia, Afghanistan, and Kashmir. For example, all the Algerians involved in Al-Qaeda came from Europe—or, like Ressam, became radicalized in Europe—and none was ever found in the strongholds of the Algerian Armed Islamic Group (GIA). The foreigners sentenced in Yemen in January 1999 for taking hostages were six British citizens of Pakistani descent, including the son-in-law of Sheykh Hamza, the Egyptian-born former imam of Finsbury Park, and two Algerians. Sheykh Saïd Omar, sentenced in Pakistan for the kidnapping of Daniel Pearl, is a British citizen born in the United Kingdom. The two young Muslims sentenced in Morocco for firing on tourists in a Marrakesh hotel in 1994 were from French Algerian families. In other words, in many cases the Islamic violence in the Middle East is imported from recommunalized Western Muslims.

The born-again Muslims of Europe are fighting at the frontiers of their imaginary ummah, and what agitates them is a consequence of their Westernization rather than any spillover from Middle Eastern conflicts. All the literature and websites linked with Al-Qaeda stress the peripheral jihad from Bosnia to the Philippines, whereas the struggles in Palestine and Iraq are not considered central—an emphasis that has been noted and criticized by some Arab militants like the Saudi Sheykh Abu Ayman al Hilali. Unsurprisingly, most of the jihadi websites are based in the West or in South Asia. This is not only because of censorship; it is also, and most importantly, because the people who are behind them are based in the West.

What Kind of Islam?

The radicalism of the terrorists has nothing to do with Islam as a culture. Neither is it the expression of the collective identity of a Muslim community. Deculturation and individualization are the two key issues in the process of radicalization, and Islam is the expression of a reconstructed self in reference to a virtual ummah. Indeed, the Islam with which such young people identify is not the cultural Islam of their parents or home countries. It is both Salafi and jihadist. Salafists seek to purge Islam of all outside influences, starting with the cultures and traditions of Muslim societies, and to restore it to the letter of the Koran as well as to the tradition of the Prophet Muhammed.

Salafism is fundamentally opposed to all cultural or national forms of Islam. By no means are all Salafists jihadists. But today's terrorists are also jihadists, since they have opted from the outset for armed struggle, which has essentially taken over the targets of the far left in the 1970s, such as United States imperialism instead of genuine support for specific national liberation movements. In fact, for many radicals, and especially the converts, activism seems to supersede religious convictions.

As mentioned already, radicalization is a consequence of the Westernization of Muslims being born and living in Europe. It is linked with a generational gap and a depressed social status, and it perpetuates a preexistent tradition of leftist, Third Worldist, anti-imperialist youth protest. Notwithstanding such radicalization, most European Muslims have found a way to conciliate faith and a non-Muslim environment in a practical, if sometimes makeshift, manner. The problem is that this de facto liberalism is not yet embedded or expressed in theological terms. This means that such liberalism is not bound into a socialization mechanism that can be transmitted easily to subsequent generations, suggesting that the present generation will remain open to radicalization.

Religion or Culture?

Neofundamentalism does not target communities with ties to a culture of origin but instead seeks out individuals in doubt about their faith and identity. It appeals to an uprooted, often young, well-educated, but frustrated and already disgruntled youth. No wonder Salafism attracts the losers of deculturation. But *loser* should not be understood in economic terms: It is not a matter of poverty but of self-identity. Salafism even made a breakthrough among an educated middle class that is not revolutionary and is looking for respectability while experiencing some sort of acculturation. In Egypt and Pakistan, for example, Salafism reaches many workers returning from the Gulf States.[2] For such uprooted individuals—whether in the West or in the Middle East—fundamentalism offers a system for regulating behavior that can fit any situation, from Afghan deserts to American college campuses. Indeed, Islam—as preached by the Taliban, Saudi Wahhabis and bin Laden's radicals—is hostile even to culture that is Muslim in origin. Whatever it has destroyed, whether Mohammad's tomb, the Buddhist Bamiyan statues in Afghanistan, or the World Trade Center, it expresses the same rejection of material civilization or culture, with Muslim cultures the first target and Western culture second. In doing so, the West is not rejected in favor of any sort of Islamic culture. Salafists do not consider Islam as a culture but as a mere religion that would lose its purity and holistic dimension if embedded in a specific culture. This is why it appeals to an unmoored second-generation youth in Europe.

Salafists dream of a tabula rasa. They do not value the classical great Muslim civilizations, such as the Umayyad or the Ottoman Empire. They reject the different religious schools as well as Sufism, which have been so instrumental in the nativization of Islam. How can we study Yemen without considering the rift between Zaydism and Shafeism or Central Asia without taking into account the role of Hanafism and Sufism? Salafists reject local Islams and wage a relentless war on folk customs and even learned traditions, religious or secular. For instance, they oppose any cult of the saints—*zyarat* in Central Asia and *moussem* in North Africa, which is a religious pilgrimage in which people come to pray to the local patron saint—and even the celebration of the Prophet's birthday, known as *mawlud*.[3] They reject Sufism and mystical practices, called *zikr,* and any form of artistic performance associated with a religious practice, such as qawwali music in Pakistan, with some exceptions, such as religious songs unaccompanied by musical instruments.[4] They reject specific burial rituals.[5] Quite evidently they also forbid participation in pagan or secular celebrations. For example, the popular Persian Nawruz festival on April 21 was banned by the Taliban; the Saudi Council of Fatwa ruled against a traditional festivity, Grayqaan or Quraiqa'an, in which children from the Gulf Coast used to knock on doors and collect treats.[6]

The Taliban, for example, went very far in their struggle against traditional Afghan culture. As is the practice of all Salafists, they first targeted bad Muslims, whereas Western culture came only second. They had rather good relations with the United States until fall 1997 and did not bother to expel Western nongovernmental organizations. Instead they took a hard line against Afghan customs and culture. They banned music, movies, dancing, and kite flying, the latter because someone climbing a tree to remove a kite might end up watching, even inadvertently, unveiled women inside the adjacent house garden. Pet songbirds were outlawed because they might have voided a believer's prayer by distracting him. The Taliban destroyed the statues of the Buddhas, not in opposition to Buddhism but—apart from Islam forbidding representation of the human form—because these statues were not linked with the current religion in Afghanistan. Even if such statues had no religious meaning, or a negative religious meaning, they would still have had to be destroyed. For the Taliban, religion should have the monopoly of the symbolic sphere. Life should be entirely devoted to prepare the individual for the hereafter, and this can be done only through abiding by a strict code of conducts and rituals.

A good example of the opposition between code and culture is food versus cuisine. Salafists do not care about cuisine. Anything that is halal is good—whatever the basic ingredients and the recipe. When they open a restaurant in the West, it never promotes Ottoman or Moroccan cuisine but instead halal food and most often will simply offer the usual Western fast food products. Similarly, halal dress can be based on Western raincoats, gloves, fashionable scarves, and so on. Halal, therefore, is a code adaptable to any culture. Objects cease to have a history and to be culturally meaningful; once chosen because they meet a normative requirement they do not refer to a specific culture. Such a view probably creates the great divide between Salafists and European opponents of American cultural hegemony. For Salafists the hamburger is seen as culturally neutral as long as it is made along the lines of a religious norm.[7] For instance, in 2003 a successful Muslim business executive in France launched a soft drink called Mecca-Cola, whose foremost quality is that it looks and tastes almost exactly like Coca-Cola, except that the marketing appeals explicitly to Islamic values and is aimed at providing support for the Palestinians.[8] Likewise, in 2004, a new fashion brand has appeared on the European market: dawa-wear, which put an Islamic logo, the stylization of a man praying, on clothes adapted to the urban youth culture.

A Religious Revival?

Salafists therefore are not interested in creating or asserting a Muslim culture. They reject the concept, even if they sometimes end up using the term to find a common language with Western societies, where the language of multiculturalism is the main idiom to deal with otherness. There is no Salafist novelist, poet, musician, filmmaker, or comedian. By stressing the gap between culture and religion and by striving to establish a pure religion separated from secular and lay elements, Salafists contribute to the paradoxical secularization of modern society, because they isolate religion from the other dimensions of social life that they would like to—but cannot—ignore or destroy. At the same time, contemporary forms of religiosity among second-generation Muslims outside the Middle East are closer to those of their nineteenth- and twentieth-century American Christian counterparts than to medieval Islam. In short, they are examples of revivalism. Religious revivalism, after all, is centered not in traditions and familial values but on individuals who experience a crisis of identity and the discontinuity of familial and communal ties. It accords with individualism; the reconstruction of an imagined community, which is the faith community or the ummah; a crisis of authority and knowledge, or defiance toward legitimate holders of religious knowledge; self-teaching; and insistence on code, values, and emotional faith more than on philosophy or abstract theology. In our time, religious revivalism is almost always socially conservative, from the American Bible Belt to the Lubavitch movement to Pope John Paul II's assault on liberation theology, a leftist and revolutionary interpretation of the Gospels. Conservative religious leaders rail against what is perceived as corruption and a loss of values. In that sense transnational European Islam is becoming a logical part of the European debate on values. Many imams preach about regaining happiness, recovering from destitution, affirming a categorical difference between right and wrong, making a good life, and so on—no different, in essence, from what Christian and Jewish clergy of orthodox orientation say to their congregations. But the people involved in global terrorism are Muslims.

It is not argued here that other religions do also produce political violence (see Mark Juergensmeyer's contribution in this book). It is clear that there is no real symmetry among Western religions, including Islam, in the translation of religious radicalism into political violence. But the specificity of Islam does not come from the Koran or from traditional Muslim political culture. It comes from contemporary Muslims, and factors pertaining to Islam are clearly linked with the social conditions of Muslims in Western Europe. For instance, almost no terrorists can be found among American second-generation Muslims.[9] This lack of radicalism is obviously linked with the difference between the two Western Muslim populations in terms of status, representation, and expectations. The Muslims in the United States are just part of a wider immigration movement of people who intend to settle in the America, whereas second-generation Muslims in Europe are the offspring of a misunderstanding: Their parents never really intend to become Europeans. In the United States Muslims are mainly middle and even upper class—the median income is higher than that of the U.S. population—whereas in Europe the rate of unemployment among second-generation Muslims is higher than the average. By the same token people with a Muslim background are overrepresented among prison inmates.[10] The U.S. radicals are mainly converts, such as Jose Padilla, the U.S. convert who was indicted in 2005 for giving support to Al Qaeda, and these converts fit precisely into the same categories of their European counterparts: racial minorities or outcasts.

A Clash of Civilizations?

The consequence is that we can speak neither of a clash nor of dialogue of cultures, because the very notion of culture is in crisis. Nevertheless, the current debate on Islam—already heavily loaded with security consideration—is still waged under the paradigm of clash–dialogue of civilizations, cultures, or religions, with all three terms largely equated. Roughly, the debate on how to fight terrorism offers two conflicting views: (1) Islam is the issue, and we are heading toward a clash of civilizations unless an in-depth reformation of Islam occurs; or (2) Islam is not the issue, and we must turn the clash into a dialogue among civilizations to address the roots of the Muslim wrath. Both positions are based on common premises: Religion is embedded in a culture, and a culture is rooted in religion, which means that the social and political behavior of believers is determined by the theological tenets of their religion. Calling for a religious reformation ignores the way believers adapt and experience their faith through practices and not through theological debates. Calling for community leaders to police their flock ignores the process of deculturation. Addressing the Middle East issues, which is a positive step in itself, ignores the deterritorialization of contemporary Islam. There is no such a thing as a Muslim community but instead a population of Muslims who have a different experience of what it means to be a Muslim—even if they share the same creed.

In Europe it is a common view to contrast two approaches, especially the British multiculturalism, where Muslims are defined by a distinct ethnocultural identity, and the French assimilation, where Muslims may become full citizens only by shedding away their pristine identity. Yet paradoxically, both approaches share the same assumptions: Religion is embedded into a culture, so that Muslims belong to a different culture. Interestingly, though, the level of radicalism has little to do with government policy: There has been as much of a terrorist threat in Great Britain, France, Spain, Belgium, and Holland, though in each of these cases the policy toward Islam is very different. The explanation is that radicals do not answer to a specific national policy but to a global perception of the state of the ummah.

In any case, both multiculturalism and assimilation failed for the same reason: Muslims in the West do not push for an ethnocultural identity but want to be recognized as a mere faith community. In Great Britain, born-again Muslims do not care about traditional culture and, thus, do not answer to traditional community leaders. Secularist France, on the other hand, was very surprised to see that the fading away of traditional Muslim culture went hand in hand with a strong religious assertiveness: the sudden veiling of some French school girls in the '90s (the "scarf affair") is not the result of an imported culture but is a consequence of the construction of a purely religious identity among educated and integrated school girls. The dominant idea in French public opinion was that cultural assimilation will go along with secularization. The concept of a noncultural religious revival was seen as unthinkable, but it happened. By creating a French Council of Muslim Faith, the government reluctantly acknowledged the existence of Islam as a mere religion.

*****

So what are the answers to the current crisis? The issue is not solving the crisis in the Middle East but accompanying the process of deculturation and assertion of Islam as a mere religion. It means making room for Islam in the West as a Western religion among others—not as the expression of an ethnocultural community. This is the real process of secularization, which has nothing to do with theological reformation but could entail a theological debate as an almost forced secularization did for the Catholic Church in continental Western Europe: The emergence of the Christian democracy—that is, the Church's full acceptation of democracy—is a consequence and not a prerequisite of the process of secularization. Political authorities should not look for traditional moderate religious thinkers from the Middle East to appease Western Muslims, nor should they spend subsidies to promote civil or liberal Islam. They should simply make room for Islam without changing laws or principles. Genuine pluralism is the best way to avoid confrontation with a Muslim population that is very diverse and that could feel coerced into a ghettoized community. As demonstrated by a host of Protestant, Catholic, and Jewish cases, conservative and even fundamentalist views of religion are manageable in a plural environment. Indeed, a pluralistic approach allows civil society to reach the youth who could be ideal targets for radicals and Salafist groups. State policy should therefore be based on integration of Muslims and community leaders on a pluralistic basis. The priority should be to weaken the links with foreign elements by pushing for the nativization of Islam and for preventing the deepening of the ghetto syndrome. Transparency and democracy are the aims.

Endnotes

1. The exception is the Kelkal networks that operated in France in 1995. They were undoubtedly linked to and manipulated by the Algerian Armed Islamic Group (GIA) (with or without some interference from the Algerian Military Security). If we consider the

motivations of the arrested militants, however, they had little to do with national solidarity with Algeria but more with a call for an overall jihad against France and the West.

2. See Muhammad Qasim Zaman, *The Ulama in Contemporary Islam: Custodians of Change* (Princeton, NJ: Princeton University Press, 2002), 148.

3. See Imaam Abdul-Azeez bin Baaz, "Fataawaa al-Islaamiyyah," the Salafi Society of North America, http://www.al-manhaj.com/Page1.cfm?ArticleID=131.

4. In Iraqi Kurdistan, the group Ansar al-Islam desecrated the graves of Sheikh Husam al-Din, Sheikh Baha al-Din, and Sheikh Siraj al-Din, known guides of the Naqishbandi order, in July 2002. The head of the group, Mullah Krekar, is a permanent resident of Norway—another good example of the relation between neofundamentalism and globalization.

5. Among others, the Pakistani custom of reciting the Koran at certain time periods after a person's death is dismissed as non-Muslim.

6. The council considered this to be a Shi'a celebration. Perhaps some of the explanation can be found in the fact that the celebration is too close to Halloween; the fact that it is more and more widely observed is another sign of globalization. It is interesting to note that the Islamic regime in Iran never banned traditional culture or nowruz, even if it demoted them in favor of religious ceremonies. After some debates, for example, Ferdowsi Street in Tehran was not renamed. In general, all Islamists acknowledge the concept of culture even if they stress its religious dimension.

7. For Muslim organizations' request to be included in a protocol of agreement with McDonald's see http://www.soundvision.com/info/mcdonalds/. For radicals' protest against the Islamic Food and Nutrition Council of America for allegedly declaring McDonald's halal, see "IFANCA Puts Label of 'Halal' on McDonald's Exports to Muslim World," *New Trend Magazine*, September 21, 2003.

8. It is interesting that one of the few attacks from Islamic militants against McDonald's did not originate with neofundamentalists but—on the contrary—from political Islamists, who still retain the concept of national heritage. Qazi Husseyn Ahmed, the leader of the Pakistani Jama'at-i Islami, said in a speech, "We will boycott them, the Pepsi and Coca Cola, and McDonald burger. This is forbidden—the Kentucky chicken and the McDonald burger is forbidden for the Muslims. There are people present here who can make such foods which are better than this McDonald burger and Kentucky chicken. Why should we allow from abroad these things?" http://www.mecca-cola.com/fr/index2.php.

9. Some of them have been indicted for their support of Hamas or Hezbollah. To me, however, there is a big difference between these two forms of political violence. Hamas and Hezbollah are Islamonationalist movements, fighting for territory and statehood. Their supporters

in the United States have a more diasporic attitude and do not act as global jihadists (see Gabriel Sheffer's contribution in this book).

10. See Farhad Khosrokhavar, *L'Islam dans les Prisons* (Paris: Balland, 2004).

Recommended Readings

Avalos, Hector. *Fighting Words: The Origins of Religious Violence.* New York: Prometheus Books, 2005.

Bell, John B. *A Time of Terror: How Democratic Societies Respond to Revolutionary Violence.* New York: Basic Books, 1978.

Bergen, Peter. *Holy War Inc.* New York: Free Press, 2002.

Bjørgo, Tore (ed.). *Root Causes of Terrorism: Myths, Realities, and Ways Forward.* New York: Routledge, 2005.

Crenshaw, Martha. *Terrorism in Context.* University Park: Pennsylvania State University Press, 1995.

Crenshaw, Martha. "The Causes of Terrorism." *Comparative Politics* 13, no. 4 (1981): 379–99. Engene, Jan Oskar. *Terrorism in Western Europe. Explaining the Trends since 1950.* Cheltenham, UK: Edward Elgar, 2004.

Esposito, John L. *The Islamic Threat: Myth or Reality?* New York: Oxford University Press, 1999.

Esposito, John L. *Unholy War: Terror in the Name of Islam.* New York: Oxford University Press, 2003.

Fuller, Graham E. *The Future of Political Islam.* New York: Palgrave MacMillan, 2003.

Gambetta, Diego (ed.). *Making Sense of Suicide Missions.* New York: Oxford University Press, 2005.

Heymann, Phil. *Terrorism Freedom and Security: Winning without War.* Cambridge, MA: MIT Press, 2003.

Horgan, John. *The Psychology of Terrorism.* New York: Routledge, 2005.

Juergensmeyer, Mark. *Terror in the Mind of God: The Global Rise of Religious Violence.* 3d ed. Berkeley: University of California Press, 2003.

Kaldor, Mary and Diego Muro. "Religious and Nationalist Militant Groups," in *Global Civil Society 2003: Yearbook,* ed. Mary Kaldor, Helmunt Anheier, and Marlies Glasius. London: LSE, 2004.

Krueger, Alan B. and Jitka Malekcová. "Education, Poverty, Political Violence and Terrorism: Is There a Causal Connection?" *Journal of Economic Perspectives* 17, no. 4 (2004): 119–44.

Lodge, Juliet (ed.). *The Threat of Terrorism.* Brighton, UK: Weatsheaf, 1988.

Mamdani, Mahmood. *Good Muslim, Bad Muslim.* New York: Columbia University Press, 2004.

McCormick, Gordon H. and Guillermo Owen. "Revolutionary Origins and Conditional Mobilization." *European Journal of Political Economy* 12 (1996): 377–402.

Pape, Robert A. *Dying to Win: The Strategic Logic of Suicide Terrorism.* New York: Random House, 2005.

Post, Jerrold M. *Leaders and Followers in a Dangerous World: The Psychology of Political Behavior.* Ithaca, NY: Cornell University Press, 2004.

Post, Jerrold M., Ehud Sprinzak, and Laurita Denny. "The Terrorists in Their Own Words: Interview with 35 Incarcerated Middle Eastern Terrorists." *Terrorism and Political Violence* 15, no. 1 (2003): 171–84.

Ross, Jeffrey Ian and Ted R. Gurr. "Why Terrorism Subsides: A Comparative Study of Canada and the United States." *Comparative Politics* 21, no. 4 (1989): 405–26.

Roy, Olivier. *Globalized Islam: The Search for a New Ummah.* New York: Columbia University Press, 2004.

Sageman, Marc. *Understanding Terror Networks.* University Park: University of Pennsylvania Press, 2004.

Schmid, Alex and Albert Jongman. *Political Terrorism: A New Guide to Actors, Authors, Concepts, Data Bases, Theories, and Literature.* New York: Transactions Publishers, 2005.

Shcholte, Jan Art. *Globalization: A Critical Introduction,* 2d ed. New York: Palgrave Palgrave MacMillan, 2005.

Sheffer, Gabriel. *Diaspora Politics: At Home Abroad.* Cambridge, UK: Cambridge University Press, 2003.

Sheffer, Gabriel. "Ethno-national Diasporas and Security." *Survival* 36, no. 1 (1994).

Veltmeyer, Henry (ed.) *Globalization and Antiglobalization: Dynamics of Change in the New World Order.* Hants, UK and Burlington, VT, USA: Ashgate, 2004.

Wardlaw, Grant. *Political Terrorism.* 2d ed. Cambridge, UK: Cambridge University Press 1989.

Weinberg, Leonard and Ami Pedahzur. *Political Parties and Terrorist Groups.* New York: Routledge, 2003.

Weinberg, Leonard and William Eubank. "Does Democracy Stimulate Terrorism?" *Terrorism and Political Violence* 6, no. 4 (1994): 417–35.

Wilkinson, Paul. *Terrorism and the Liberal State.* New York: New York University Press, 1979.

About the International Summit on Democracy, Terrorism, and Security

March 11, 2004

Ten bombs exploded on four trains during rush hour in Madrid. More than 190 people died, almost 2,000 were injured. It was one of the most devastating terrorist attacks in Europe in recent history. As in the United States of America on September 11, 2001, it was an attack on freedom and democracy by an international network of terrorists.

One year on, Madrid was the setting for a unique conference, the International Summit on Democracy, Terrorism, and Security. Its purpose was to build a common agenda on how the community of democratic nations can most effectively confront terrorism, in memory of its victims from across the world.

Objectives

The Madrid Summit aimed to promote a vision of a world founded on democratic values and committed to effective cooperation in the fight against terrorism. It brought together the world's leading scholars, practitioners, and most influential policymakers. It was the largest gathering of security and terrorism experts that has ever taken place:

- Twenty-three serving Heads of State and Government.
- Thirty-four former Heads of State and Government.
- Official Delegations from more than sixty countries.
- Heads of inter-governmental and international organizations including the United Nations, the European Parliament, Council and Commission, NATO, Interpol, the League of Arab States, and many others.

- 200 experts on terrorism and security.
- 500 representatives from non-governmental organizations and civil society.

Results

The principal legacy of the Madrid Summit is an innovative plan of action, the Madrid Agenda, which was adopted by an Extraordinary General Assembly of the Club de Madrid on March 11, 2005. It draws on the contributions made at the Summit, in particular the speeches given by the leaders of official delegations, the discussions that took place during more than twenty panel sessions, and—most importantly—the papers delivered by members of the expert working groups.

The Working Groups

In the months leading up to the Madrid Summit, more than 200 of the world's leading scholars and expert practitioners explored the issues of democracy, terrorism, and security in an unparalleled process of scholarly debate. The discussions were conducted through a system of password-protected web-logs. On the first day of the summit, the groups met in closed sessions to conclude their discussions.

Of the seventeen working groups, five dealt with the causes and underlying factors of terrorism. Some of the most noteworthy papers produced by individual members of these groups are reproduced in this book.

Psychology

- Jerrold Post, George Washington University, USA (coordinator)
- Scott Atran, University of Michigan, USA, and Centre National de la Recherche Scientifique, France
- Dipak Gupta, San Diego State University, USA
- Nasra Hasan, United Nations Information Service
- John Horgan, University College Cork, Ireland
- Ariel Merari, Tel Aviv University, Israel
- Marc Sageman, Foreign Policy Research Institute, USA
- Alex Schmid, United Nations Office for Drugs and Crime
- Chris Stout, University of Illinois, USA
- Jeff Victoroff, University of Southern California, USA
- Stevan Weine, University of Illinois, USA

Political Factors

- Martha Crenshaw, Wesleyan University, USA (coordinator)
- Rogelio Alonso, Universidad Rey Juan Carlos, Spain
- Mohamed Fared Azzi, Oran University, Algeria
- Ronald Crelinsten, University of Ottawa, Canada
- José Luis Herrero, FRIDE Foundation, Spain
- Barbara Lethem Ibrahim, Population Council, Egypt
- Saad Eddin Ibrahim, American University Cairo, Egypt
- Fernando Reinares, Universidad Rey Juan Carlos, Spain
- Ignacio Sánchez-Cuenca, Instituto Juan March, Spain
- Ekaterina Stepanova, Russian Academy of Sciences
- Mario Sznajder, Hebrew University, Israel
- Leonard Weinberg, University of Nevada, USA

Economic Factors

- Ted Gurr, University of Maryland, USA (coordinator)
- Alberto Abadie, Harvard University, USA
- Jose Antonio Alonso, Universidad Complutense de Madrid, Spain
- Tore Bjorgo, Norwegian Police University College (deputy coordinator)
- Yigal Carmon, Middle East Media Research Institute, USA
- Sue Eckert, Brown University, USA
- David Gold, New School University, New York, USA
- Atanas Gotchev, University of National and World Economy, Bulgaria
- Jeroen Gunning, University of Aberystwyth, Wales
- Jitka Maleckova, Charles University, Czech Republic
- Lyubov Mincheva, University of Sofia, Bulgaria
- Alex Schmid, United Nations Office for the Prevention of International Terrorism (advisory)
- Gabriel Sheffer, Hebrew University of Jerusalem, Israel
- Joshua Sinai, independent researcher, USA
- Michael Stohl, University of California at Santa Barbara, USA
- Ekkart Zimmermann, Dresden University of Technology, Germany

Religion

- Mark Juergensmeyer, University of California at Santa Barbara, USA (coordinator)
- Jalal Al-Mashta, Al-Nahdhah newspaper, Iraq
- Azyumardi Azra, State Islamic University, Indonesia

- Dalil Boubaker, French Muslim Council
- Antonio Elorza, Universidad Complutense de Madrid, Spain
- John Esposito, Georgetown University, USA
- Dru Gladney, University of Hawaii/ East-West Center, USA
- Samuel Peleg, Strategic Dialogue Centre Israel
- Harish Puri, Guru Nanak Dev University, India
- Ian Reader, Lancaster University, England
- David Rosen, American Jewish Committee
- Behzad Shahndeh, Tehran University, Iran
- Susumu Shimazono, Tokyo University, Japan
- Shibley Telhami, University of Maryland, USA
- Bassam Tibbi, Göttingen University, Germany

Culture

- Jessica Stern, Harvard University, USA (coordinator)
- Nabi Abdullaev, The Moscow Times, Russia
- Hassan Abbas, Harvard Law School, USA
- Haizam Amirah Fernandez, Real Instituto Elcano, Spain
- Mark Beissinger, University of Wisconsin, USA
- Ejaz Haider, The Friday Times, Pakistan
- Gilles Kepel, Institut d'Etudes Politiques, France
- Jean-Luc Marret, Fondation pour la Recherche Strategique, France
- Andres Ortega, El Pais, Spain
- Gardner Peckham, BKSH, USA
- Olivier Roy, Centre National de la Recherche Scientifique, France
- Giandomenico Picco, GDP Associates, USA

The Madrid Agenda

To remember and honour the victims of the terrorist attacks of March 11, 2004, the strength and courage of the citizens of Madrid, and through them, all victims of terrorism and those who confront its threat.

We, the members of the Club de Madrid, former Presidents and Prime Ministers of democratic countries dedicated to the promotion of democracy, have brought together political leaders, experts, and citizens from across the world.

We listened to many voices. We acknowledged the widespread fear and uncertainty generated by terrorism. Our principles and policy recommendations address these fundamental concerns.

Ours is a call to action for leaders everywhere. An agenda for action for governments, institutions, civil society, the media, and individuals. A global democratic response to the global threat of terrorism.

The Madrid Principles

Terrorism is a crime against all humanity. It endangers the lives of innocent people. It creates a climate of hate and fear. It fuels global divisions along ethnic and religious lines. Terrorism constitutes one of the most serious violations of peace, international law, and the values of human dignity.

Terrorism is an attack on democracy and human rights. No cause justifies the targeting of civilians and non-combatants through intimidation and deadly acts of violence.

We firmly reject any ideology that guides the actions of terrorists. We decisively condemn their methods. Our vision is based on a common set of universal values and principles. Freedom and human dignity. Protection and empowerment of citizens. Building and strengthening of democracy at all levels. Promotion of peace and justice.

A Comprehensive Response

We owe it to the victims to bring the terrorists to justice. Law enforcement agencies need the powers required, yet they must never sacrifice the principles they are meant to defend. Measures to counter terrorism should fully respect international standards of human rights and the rule of law.

In the fight against terrorism, forceful measures are necessary. Military action, when needed, must always be coordinated with law enforcement and judicial measures, as well as political, diplomatic, economic, and social responses.

We call upon every state to exercise its right and fulfill its duty to protect its citizens. Governments, individually and collectively, should prevent and combat terrorist acts. International institutions, governments, and civil society should also address the underlying risk factors that provide terrorists with support and recruits.

International Cooperation

Terrorism is now a global threat. We saw it not only in Madrid, New York, and Washington, but also in Dar-es-Salaam, Nairobi, Tel Aviv, Bali, Riyadh, Casablanca, Baghdad, Bombay, and Beslan. It calls for a global response. Governments and civil society must reignite their efforts at promoting international engagement, cooperation, and dialogue.

International legitimacy is a moral and practical imperative. A multilateral approach is indispensable. International institutions, especially the United Nations, must be strengthened. We must renew our efforts to make these institutions more transparent, democratic, and effective in combating the threat.

Narrow national mindsets are counterproductive. Legal institutions, law enforcement, and intelligence agencies must cooperate and exchange pertinent information across national boundaries.

Citizens and Democracy

Only freedom and democracy can ultimately defeat terrorism. No other system of government can claim more legitimacy, and through no other system can political grievances be addressed more effectively.

Citizens promote and defend democracy. We must support the growth of democratic movements in every nation, and reaffirm our commitment to solidarity, inclusiveness, and respect for cultural diversity.

Citizens are actors, not spectators. They embody the principles and values of democracy. A vibrant civil society plays a strategic role in protecting local communities, countering extremist ideologies, and dealing with political violence.

A Call to Action

An aggression on any nation is an aggression on all nations. An injury to one human being is an injury to all humanity. Indifference cannot be countenanced. We call on each and everyone. On all States, all organizations—national and international. On all citizens.

Drawing on the deliberations of political leaders, experts, and citizens, we have identified the following recommendations for action, which we believe should be extended, reviewed, and implemented as part of an ongoing, dynamic process.

The Madrid Recommendations

Political and philosophical differences about the nature of terrorism must not be used as an excuse for inaction. We support the Global Strategy for Fighting Terrorism announced by the Secretary General of the United Nations at the Madrid Summit on March 10. We urgently call for:

- the adoption of the definition proposed by the United Nations High-Level Panel on Threats, Challenges and Change.
- the ratification and implementation of all terrorism-related conventions by those states which have not yet done so.

- the speedy conclusion of the Comprehensive Convention on International Terrorism.

And we believe it is a moral and practical necessity to address the needs of terrorist victims. We therefore recommend:

- the exploration of the possibility of creating high commissioners for victims both at the international and the national level, who will represent the victims' right to know the truth, as well as obtain justice, adequate redress, and integral reparation.

International Cooperation

The basis for effective cooperation across national borders is trust and respect for the rule of law. Trust is built through shared norms, reciprocity and the practical experience of effective collaboration. To encourage this sense of mutual confidence, we propose:

- the establishment of regular, informal forums for law enforcement and intelligence officials, which may grow from bilateral consultations into a formalized structure for multilateral cooperation.
- the strengthening of regional organizations, so that measures to combat terrorism are tailored to local needs and benefit from local knowledge and networks.
- the effective coordination of these mechanisms at the global level.

International collaboration in the fight against terrorism is also a question of human and financial capital. We call for:

- the establishment of an international mechanism—including states, non-governmental organizations, and the private sector—to help link states that are in need of resources with those that can provide assistance.
- the creation of a trust fund for the purpose of assisting governments that lack the financial resources to implement their obligations, as proposed by the United Nations High-Level Panel.

Underlying Risk Factors

Terrorism thrives on intimidation, fear, and hatred. While authorities have a responsibility to ensure freedom, including religious freedom, leaders, including religious leaders, have a responsibility not to abuse that freedom by encouraging or justifying hatred, fanaticism, or religious war. We propose:

- the systematic promotion of cultural and religious dialogue through local encounters, round tables, and international exchange programs.
- the continuous review by authorities and the mass media of their use of language, to ensure it does not unwittingly or disproportionately reinforce the terrorist objective of intimidation, fear, and hatred.
- the creation of programs, national and international, to monitor the expression of racism, ethnic confrontation, and religious extremism and their impact in the media, as well as to review school textbooks for their stance on cultural and religious tolerance.

While poverty is not a direct cause of terrorism, economic and social policy can help mitigate exclusion and the impact of rapid socioeconomic change, which give rise to grievances that are often exploited by terrorists. We recommend:

- the adoption of long-term trade, aid, and investment policies that help empower marginalized groups and promote participation.
- new efforts to reduce structural inequalities within societies by eliminating group discrimination.
- the launch of programs aimed at promoting women's education, employment, and empowerment.
- the implementation of the Millennium Development Goals by 2015.

Terrorists prosper in societies where there are unresolved conflicts and few accountable mechanisms for addressing political grievances. We call for:

- new initiatives at mediation and peace-making for societies which are marked by conflict and division, because democracy and peace go hand in hand.
- a redoubling of efforts to promote and strengthen democratic institutions and transparency within countries and at the global level. Initiatives such as the Community of Democracies may contribute to this goal.

Confronting Terrorism

Democratic principles and values are essential tools in the fight against terrorism. Any successful strategy for dealing with terrorism requires terrorists to be isolated. Consequently, the preference must be to treat terrorism as criminal acts to be handled through existing systems of law enforcement and with full respect for human rights and the rule of law. We recommend:

- taking effective measures to make impunity impossible either for acts of terrorism or for the abuse of human rights in counter-terrorism measures.
- the incorporation of human rights laws in all anti-terrorism programs and policies of national governments as well as international bodies.
- The implementation of the proposal to create a special rapporteur who would report to the United Nations Commission on Human Rights on the compatibility of counter-terrorism measures with human rights law, as endorsed by the United Nations Secretary General in Madrid.
- the inclusion and integration of minority and diaspora communities in our societies.
- the building of democratic political institutions across the world embodying these same principles.

In the fight against terrorism, any information about attacks on another state must be treated like information relating to attacks on one's own state. In order to facilitate the sharing of intelligence across borders, we propose:

- the overhaul of classification rules that hinder the rapid exchange of information.
- the clarification of conditions under which information will be shared with other states on the basis of availability.
- the use of state-of-the-art technology to create regional and global anti-terrorism databases.

The principle of international solidarity and cooperation must also apply to defensive measures. We recommend:

- the creation of cross-border preparedness programs in which governments and private business participate in building shared stockpiles of pharmaceuticals and vaccines, as well as the seamless cooperation of emergency services.

Solidarity must be enhanced by new efforts at coordinating the existing instruments of anti-terrorist collaboration. We propose:

- the streamlining and harmonization of national and international tools in the fight against terrorism.
- the creation of clear guidelines on the role of the armed forces in relation to other agencies of law enforcement at the national level.
- the drawing up of national plans to coordinate responsibilities in the fight against terrorism, allowing for agencies or organizations with special skills to contribute to a comprehensive effort.

The threat from terrorism has made efforts to limit the proliferation of weapons of mass destruction even more urgent. We call for:

- the United Nations Security Council to initiate on-site investigations where it is believed that a state is supporting terrorist networks, and if necessary to use the full range of measures under Chapter VII of the United Nations Charter.
- the conclusion of the International Convention for the Suppression of Acts of Nuclear Terrorism, and the strengthening and implementation of the biological weapons convention.
- the continuation of innovative global efforts to reduce the threat from weapons of mass destruction, such as the Global Threat Reduction Initiative and the Global Partnerships.

Terrorists must be deprived of the financial resources necessary to conduct their campaigns. To curb terrorist funding networks, we recommend:

- increased and coordinated law enforcement and political and civic education campaigns aimed at reducing the trafficking of illegal narcotics, revenues from which are used to finance terrorism.
- the creation of an international anti-terrorist finance center, which furthers research, trains national enforcement officials, and serves as a source of coordination and mutual assistance.
- the development of tools to increase the transparency of fundraising in the private and charitable sectors through the exchange of best practices.

- the expansion of 'financial intelligence units', which facilitate the effective corporation between government agencies and financial institutions.

Civil Society

The process of building democracy as an antidote to terrorism and violence needs to be supported by the international community and its citizens. We propose:

- The creation of a global citizens network, linking the leaders of civil society at the forefront of the fight for democracy from across the world, taking full advantage of web-based technologies and other innovative forms of communication.

- An 'early warning system' as part of this network, helping to defuse local conflicts before they escalate, as well as providing a channel for moral and material support to civil society groups facing repression.

Club de Madrid
Madrid, March 11, 2005

About the Club de Madrid

Mission

The Club de Madrid is an independent organization dedicated to strengthening democracy around the world. It launches global initiatives, conducts projects, and acts as a consultative body for governments, democratic leaders, and institutions involved in processes of democratic transition. The personal practical experience of its members—fifty-seven former heads of state and government—in processes of democratic transition and consolidation is the Club de Madrid's unique resource. Along with the experience and cooperation of other high level political practitioners and governance experts, this resource is a working tool to convert ideas into practical recommendations.

Programs and Activities

The Club de Madrid brings three major resources to its work:

- A unique mix of former heads of state and government.
- A committed focus on democratic transition and consolidation.
- Programs with a practical approach and measurable results.

The Club de Madrid undertakes projects related to its core mission of promoting and defending democracy. One of the Club de Madrid's major assets is the ability of its members to offer strategic advice and peer-to-peer counsel to current leaders striving to build or consolidate democracy. The organization also plays an advocacy role in promoting democratic principles in certain country, regional, or thematic cases, such as with the International Summit on Democracy, Terrorism and Security.

To learn more about the Club de Madrid's mission and activities, please go to its website—www.clubmadrid.org—or contact the Club directly:

Club de Madrid
Felipe IV, 9 – 3° izqda.
28014 Madrid
Spain
Tel: +34 91 523 72 16
Fax: +34 91 532 00 88
Email: clubmadrid@clubmadrid.org

Members of the Club de Madrid

Adamkus, Valdas (on leave)   President of Lithuania
Aho, Esko   Former Prime Minister of Finland
Ahtisaari, Martti   Former President of Finland   .
Alfonsín, Raúl   Former President of Argentina
Al Mahdi, Sadig   Former Prime Minister of Sudan
Arzú, Alvaro   Former President of Guatemala
Aylwin, Patricio   Former President of Chile
Aznar, José María   Former Prime Minister of Spain
Betancur, Belisario   Former President of Colombia
Bildt, Carl   Former Prime Minister of Sweden
Birkavs, Valdis   Former Prime Minister of Latvia
Bondevik, Kjell Magne   Former Prime Minister of Norway
Brundtland, Gro Harlem   Former Prime Minister of Norway
Calvo Sotelo, Leopoldo   Former Prime Minister of Spain
Campbell, Kim   Former Prime Minister of Canada; Secretary-General of the Club de Madrid
Cardoso, Fernando Henrique   Former President of Brazil; President of the Club de Madrid
Cavaco Silva, Aníbal   Former Prime Minister of Portugal
Chissano, Joaquim   Former President of Mozambique
Clinton, William J.   Former President of the United States of America, Honorary Co-Chair of the Club de Madrid
Delors, Jacques   Former President of the European Commission
Dimitrov, Philip   Former Prime Minister of Bulgaria
El Eryani, Abdulkarim   Former Prime Minister of Yemen
Fernández, Leonel (on leave)   President of the Dominican Republic
Figueres, José María   Former President of Costa Rica
Finnbogadottír, Vigdís   Former President of Iceland
Frei Ruiz-Tagle, Eduardo   Former President of Chile
Gaviria, César   Former President of Colombia
González Márquez, Felipe   Former Prime Minister of Spain

Gorbachev, Mikhail Former President of the Soviet Union
Gujral, Inder Kumar Former Prime Minister of India
Guterres, António Former Prime Minister of Portugal
Havel, Václav Former President of Czechoslovakia and of the Czech Republic
Hurtado, Osvaldo Former President of Ecuador
Jospin, Lionel Former Prime Minister of France
Kohl, Helmut Former Chancellor of Germany
Kok, Wim Former Prime Minister of the Netherlands
Konare, Alpha Oumar Former President of Mali
Kučan, Milan Former President of Slovenia
Lacalle Herrera, Luis Alberto Former President of Uruguay
Lagos, Ricardo President of Chile (after completion of mandate)
Lagumdžija, Zlatko Former Prime Minister of Bosnia and Herzegovina
Lee, Hong Koo Former Prime Minister of Korea
Major, John Sir Former Prime Minister of the United Kingdom
Mascarenhas Monteiro, Antonio M. Former President of Cape Verde
Masire, Ketumile Former President of Botswana
Mazowiecki, Tadeusz Former Prime Minister of Poland
Meidani, Rexhep Former President of the Republic of Albania
Meri, Lennart Former President of Estonia
Mkapa, Benjamin President of Tanzania (after completion of mandate)
Paniagua, Valentín Former President of Peru
Panyarachun, Anand Former Prime Minister of Thailand
Pastrana, Andrés Former President of Colombia
Pérez de Cuéllar, Javier Former Prime Minister of Peru
Prodi, Romano Former President of the EC, Former Prime Minister of Italy
Quiroga, Jorge Former President of Bolivia
Ramos, Fidel Valdes Former President of the Republic of the Philippines
Rasmussen, Poul Nyrup Former Prime Minister of Denmark
Robinson, Mary Former President of Ireland, Vice-President of the Club de Madrid
Roman, Petre Former Prime Minister of Romania
Sampaio, Jorge Fernando Branco de President of Portugal (after completion of mandate)
Sánchez de Lozada, Gonzalo Former President of Bolivia
Sanguinetti, Julio María Former President of Uruguay
Shipley, Jennifer Mary Former Prime Minister of New Zealand
Soares, Mario Former President of Portugal
Suárez, Adolfo Former Prime Minister of Spain

Suchocka, Hanna   Former Prime Minister of Poland
Uteem, Cassam   Former President of Mauritius
Zedillo, Ernesto   Former President of Mexico

Honorary Members

Aguirre, Esperanza   President of the Regional Government of Madrid
Carter, Jimmy   Former President of the United States of America
Rodríguez Zapatero, José Luis   Prime Minister of Spain
Ruiz Gallardón, Alberto   Mayor of the City of Madrid

Index

Iraqi Kurdistan, 121
Ireland. *See* Northern Ireland
Irish Republican Army, 50, 63, 73,
     87, 121
  funding of, 94
Islam, 7, 134
  acceptance of, 8
  European, 161
  financing of terrorism by, 37
  ideological principles derived
     from, 91
  militants, 33
  relationship of to terror, 145
  suicide operations of, 30
Islamic Front for Jihad against Jews
     and Crusaders, 154
Islamic Jihad, 23, 121, 124, 137, 149.
     See also Palestinian Islamic
     Jihad
  Egyptian, 24
  suicide bombers, 30
Islamic militants, 159. *See also*
     extremist organizations
Islamic mysticism, 146
Islamic radicalism, 148
Islamic terrorism, 135
Israel, 45, 92, 121
  displacement of West Bank
     Palestinians by, 20
  occupation of West Bank and
     Gaza Strip, 48
  suicide operations in, 133
Israeli Olympic village seizure, 17
Israeli-Palestinian conflict, 11, 48,
     53, 127, 137, 151
  use of suicide bombing in, 156
     (*See also* suicide bombing)
Italy, 46, 48
  amnesty programs for group exit
     in, 27
  bombings in, 77
  Christian Democrats, 50
  fascist regime in, 80
  Prima Linea, 4 (*See also* Prima
     Linea)
  Red Brigades, 4 (*See also* Red
     Brigades)
  revolutionary terrorism in, 74

terrorist groups in, 78 (*See also*
     specific groups)
ITERATE III, 52

J

Jaish e Mohammad, 34
Jammu, 53. *See also* Kashmir
Japan, 52
  Aum Shinrikyo movement in, 138,
     140
  fascist regime in, 80
  nerve gas attacks in, 138
  revolutionary terrorism in, 76
Jewish terrorist groups, 124, 133
  Messianic movements, 140
Jews, 124, 126
Jihad, 7, 135, 145, 155
  interpretation of, 149
  link with militancy and
     madrassas, 34
  material gain and, 93
  peripheral, 162
  suicide bombers, 3, 33
Jihadist doctrines, 91
Jordan, 65, 119
Judaism, 135

K

Kach, 124
Kahane Chai, 124
Kahane, Rabbi Meir, 124, 134
Kashmir, 11, 41, 53, 94, 121, 150
  Muslim separatist movement in,
     140
  oppression and liberation of
     Muslims in, 147
  suicide operations in, 31, 33
Kazakhstan, 66
Kenya, truck bombings in, 154
Kharajites, 150
Khomeini, Ayatollah, 149
Kosovo, 90, 95, 121, 150
Kurdish-Turkish conflict, 127
Kurdistan, 121
  Workers' Party, 22 (*See also* PKK)